Dear Dr. Price

A Letter to My Pastor

Olivia Thompson Green, Ph.D.

Dear Dr. Price a Letter to My Pastor
By Dr. Olivia Thompson Green

Published by Inflight Publishing House
5600 Harcourt Ave.
Los Angeles, California 90043

Email:otgreen5@yahoo.com
website: otgreen.net

Library of Congress Control Number: 2011911646
International Standard Book Number: 978-0-9829830-0-3

Unless otherwise noted, all Scripture quotations are from the King James Version of the Bible.

First Edition
First Printing July 2011

Cover Design by George Hooks
Packaging by Tommie Hayden
Interior Design: Caldonia Joyce
                Visual Bridge Designs
                www.VisualBridgeDesigns.com

Distributed by Professional Business Consultants
Dr.Rosie@Dr.Rosie.com

Printed in the United States of America

Table of Contents

This book is in loving memory of:

My deceased husband,
Rodney Kevin Mitchell,
~: :~
My loving father,
Oliver Nathaniel Thompson
~: :~
My devoted Grandmother,
Alberta James Shivers.

Special thanks, with deep appreciation and love, to:
my husband of over twenty-six years, Charles A. Green,
for his encouragement to me to finish writing this book and
his assistance in the completion of it.

Thank you, to my special friend,
Kenneth B. Childs, for always being there.

To my son, Howard W. Harriston (Musa), and
my daughters, Toi R. Green and Wynter H. Green,
thank you and I love you.

Thank you and I love you, to
my sisters, Johnnie Shivers and Patrice Conway,
my cousins, Augustine Kincy, LaVera Facey,
Tracy Morrison and Sherri Franklin,
my aunt, Cithy Newman, and
my other mother, Edith Meiszner.

To my other family members and friends new and old,
Tasleem Dawud, Paula Cherry, Bobbie Saul and Robert E. Rubin
who encouraged me, prayed with and for me, partied with me,
cried with me and mourned with me,
I love you and thank you.

Special thanks to
Apostle Beverly BAM Crawford, Pastor James E. Price, and
Dr. Deloris Jones.

And to my Queen Mother, Dr. Betty Price,
a special heart filled appreciation for your guidance and
example of a loving, caring wife, mother and godly woman.

Special Dedication

Dear Apostle Fredrick K. C. Price,

Greetings to you in the Name of our Lord and Savior Jesus Christ! As a result of your teaching ministry and the support ministries of Crenshaw Christian Center, I have matured and accepted God's purpose for my life.

It has taken me over twenty-five years of living and spiritual growth to develop the confidence I needed to complete this book. You and your beautiful wife, Dr. Betty Price, are examples of a whole and loving Christian married couple.

After my husband, Charles, found my handwritten letter to you, he read it and encouraged me to not only finish it, but said it should be converted into a book. I prayed and asked God for directions. Enclosed is my testimony of faith and of how trusting in God's Word empowered me to overcome impossible odds in my walk of faith.

Your obedience to God's Word and the revelation of that Word has had a domino effect in many lives all over the world. I am just one of those lives, and this is my story.

Sincerely,
Dr. Olivia Thompson Green

INTRODUCTION

What started out as a testimonial letter to Apostle Price has grown and developed into a book. This book is written to both women and men, Christian and non Christian, young and old. This book is filled with a short period of the accomplishments in my life as a result of *walking by faith*. Walking by faith is not just a cliché, but it is a mind set.

Walking by faith is a way of life.

Your attitude must change by the renewing of your mind. And the renewing of your mind happens when you study and obey the Word of God. Not only is there eternal life in your obedience to God's written and revealed Word, but also God's provision for you in this life.

To the readers of my journey that call upon the Name of Jesus Christ, my desire is that your faith is stimulated and developed so that you, too, can live whole and in the full obedience of God's Word. Walk in the Fruit of the Spirit so that God can be glorified through your life.

To those readers who are living in double-mindedness, stop procrastinating and step on over to God's side. Otherwise, your mountain will never come down, and you will never get out of that valley. Be either hot or cold, not lukewarm. You know what I'm talking about.

Stop trying God and TRUST GOD!

And, to the readers who have not made a quality decision to give their life to God through Jesus Christ, I say, "Been there!" I quote PSALMS 34:8;

> "O taste and see that the Lord is good. . ."

Occasionally, you will see the word

Pause!

This is used as the biblical word Selah is used.
Take a moment and think about what you just read.

Meditate on it.

Chapter 1

Jehovah Shalom
The Giver of my Peace
Judges 6:24

$\mathcal{M}$y story begins on Thursday, March 18, 1982. My husband, at that time, was a born again Christian, at least that's what he told me before we were married. As the result of cocaine and other mind altering things, my husband, unfortunately, became a slave to these demons and that led to his death.

He came home from his office about 1:00 p.m. in the afternoon. He was a young entrepreneur and part owner of a car business in Los Angeles, California. This particular afternoon he walked into the study where I was sitting, reached over and gave me a juicy kiss on my lips.

Coming home in the middle of the day was not any thing unusual, for him, but what was alarming to me was the dream I had the night before.

My husband was a very handsome man in his mid-twenties. He stood just under six feet tall with a great build. He was a proud man with an air of confidence and success. He was extremely intelligent and organized. He was so organized, he kept an appointment book and a daily journal.

He enjoyed politics and was a conservative Republican with a strong interest in Watergate. Nixon and Watergate mesmerized him to the degree that he bought every book he could find written on the subject.

Both his home office and business office were decorated with class. The home office was elegant 70s and the business office was a Queen Ann style setting with cherrywood furnishings.

My husband drove a silver, 280 SEL Mercedes and I drove an inside and outside powder blue Cadillac Seville. He wore a suit and tie every day and carried a briefcase.

My husband had a warm and caring smile with gentle hands. He was a loyal friend. But don't cross him or he would become your worse nightmare. He was a family man who loved his parents and siblings. He had only one sister and he loved her dearly.

During our courtship, he embraced my son as his own and they became the best of friends. My husband and my son would play tennis on the weekends. He would take my son to the car auctions so he could see where he bought cars and how the business worked. This man was wonderful and caring.

I divorced my son's natural father before my son turned two. To tell the truth, my family was not in support of me getting married at all, and especially at such a young age. To make matters worse, I was still in high school.

I was in my senior year of high school when my mother put me out of the house. My father's sister and her husband lived next door to where we lived, so I moved in with them. I met my son's father at a get-high gathering. I was friends with his cousin. Upon our first meeting, our moment began.

Actually, I didn't need my parent's consent or even their approval to marry. I was eighteen and in the first generation to become a legal adult, and be able to vote at eighteen. My son's natural father and I went downtown to the Los Angeles courthouse with two friends and my baptism certificate and said our I dos.

I didn't marry because I was pregnant, I got married in order to get pregnant and present my father with a grandchild. Having babies out of wedlock was not an option for me or my sister. When it came to having children, my daddy said, "Marry first."

Remember, back in the 60s and 70s we wore natural hair and we were black and proud. My son's father was on the short side but well built. His complexion was very light, plus he had blue/green eyes, and sported a big blond natural.

Some would say he was fine. In my eyes, yes! He was. He looked well dressed on the outside but later on, I found out that he had no substance inside.

If I had only known that our first date was financed by his aging grandmother, I might have thought twice about starting a relationship with this man. For what it's worth, the sex was good, and he always had a supply of good weed to smoke. Not the best idea for starting a relationship. What do you think?

The added motivation for my getting married was my father walking in on us in bed. At that time in my life, except for sex, I was really inexperienced about being on my own, and the responsibilities connected with being on my own. I had never worked a job and knew nothing about paying bills. My father's thought was, if I got a taste of making my own money, it would cause me to drop out of school.

So, while in high school I never pursued employment. But deep down inside, I knew that I was getting ready to hit the real world and I would need stability. All I knew was family. My father also told me, "If you marry a bum, be willing to take care of him." My father must have seen something I didn't see. Was he preparing me for something?

After the first three months of marriage, I realized the difference between a real man and a male. My son's father was a Viet Nam veteran. Although he survived Viet Nam and returned home in one piece, his mind was broken and he lived in fragments of reality. He couldn't make up his mind about his future or the future of his young family. He couldn't make up his mind whether to attend school or not; or to get a job and work or not. By the time I was seven months pregnant, I wanted out of the marriage. At this point in my life, my father's words came back to haunt me. "If you marry a bum, be willing to take care of him."

I was still very young, but I couldn't see myself working hard and taking care of a grown man. My father had to beg me to stay with him at least until the baby was born. My father told me my son was the only good thing my son's father ever gave me.

It was the influence of other men in my son's life that modeled manhood for him. My new husband was one of those influential men. He had such potential, he could have become a councilman or senator, or who knows, even the president of the United States of America. My son was so impressed with his new step-father, he started emulating him, wearing ties and jackets. He even carried a briefcase to elementary school.

Let's go back to the night before my husband's death. It was very alarming to me. I was already concerned when my husband came home because it was late. I hoped he was coming from his business and not from the dope house. I was in the bedroom when he walked in and sat down in the big, brown, Queen Ann style chair.

He had an extremely distressed look on his face. I asked him if everything was all right. He said, "Everything is good." He added there were things on his mind but I was not to worry. He was like that, always concerned for my well being.

While he was sitting in the chair, I was sitting up in the bed. He reassured me that everything was fine and requested that I lie back and go to sleep. As I sat on the bed, still looking at him, I reached over for the remote control to change the channel on the television, barely taking my eyes off of him for two seconds. What I'm about to say might sound unbelievable, but when I looked back to him, I saw the most hideous creature or spirit sitting in the chair. I blinked my eyes in unbelief and called his name. As I finished pronouncing his name, whatever I saw disappeared. With a cool, blank face he glanced up and answered me, "Yes!"

Then he stood up from the chair and walked towards me. He leaned over and kissed me good night. He walked out of the bedroom with a perplexed look on his face. I asked him, "Where are you going?" He said, "The next room, my office."

The coldness in his voice gave me chills. Now I'm really afraid, but I didn't say anything to him. I laid back in the bed, got under the covers and started praying softly in the understanding and in the Spirit.

In the understanding I prayed, "God please protect me and my son from harm." I took authority over the spirit that was hovering over my husband. Eventually, I nodded out and went to sleep.

Looking back on that night, my husband never came to bed. He slept fully dressed on the burgundy, six foot long sofa in his office. That was the beginning of many long nights of prayer for protection.

In my dream, my husband was shot and killed. I woke up terrified. This is where God's peace stepped in, and where there is peace, there is no fear. I started praying and soon, was again asleep. Remember, God will not permit more than we can bear and God will not allow calamity to catch us off guard.

I got up the next morning at my usual time to get my son ready and off to school. My husband was still asleep in his office. I didn't want to wake him, but we always had coffee together before he left for work. Because of the dream, this morning was different. I knew something was going to happen, I just didn't know what or how.

I waited until he got up, served him coffee and asked if he was hungry. With a fakeness in his voice, he said no thank you, he would eat later.

Normally, we would select and agree together on what clothing he would wear, but like I said, this morning was different. Instead, I chose a shirt, suit and tie for the day by myself. While he showered, I laid out his underwear, matched his socks and shined his shoes. We had our last cup of coffee together and he left. I started praying in the spirit for guidance.

I called my father-in-law and tried to convey to him that something disastrous was going to happen. I pleaded with him, "Please, talk to your son."

My father-in-law tried to assure me that everything was okay, but I knew in my spirit things were not okay. The spirit of death was on the prowl and I believed in my heart that my husband was his intended target.

After talking with my father-in-law, I was still troubled by my dream. I had no peace in my spirit about my husband. Nevertheless, the day was beautiful. The day was sunny, no clouds in the sky, not too hot, not too cold, just right.

I walked to the back yard so I could pray. I enjoyed hearing the birds singing and viewing the magnificence of the trees. All

I knew to do was to pray, so I did. I went into intercession not knowing I was praying to fortify myself for what was about to happen.

I was outdoors in the back yard standing on the grass, when my husband came out and asked me what I was doing. I said, "I'm praying and just enjoying the sun." I was a stay-at-home mom and he knew I would spend time during the day in prayer. I asked him if he was hungry. He told me that he had stopped by his mother's house and had some gumbo. He asked if I was hungry. I said no.

He turned and walked toward the house. I turned to follow him. He was in front and I was about three steps behind. He walked up the four steps through my son's bedroom into the hallway to his home office and sat in his big, black swivel chair behind the desk.

I entered the room behind him and sat on the burgundy sofa. He made a phone call while I turned the television on low and tried to focus on the program. In a flash, he got up from his desk and walked out of the study. I got up immediately and followed him. He walked down the hall, passing through the dining room to the kitchen for a drink of water.

By now, I'm following him around the house stepping on his heels like a small puppy. After the drink of water, he walked back to the dining room and checked the mail slot. The mail was in. He sat down at the table and started reading through the mail.

At the time, I thought it strange that the Spirit of God would prompt me to get fully dressed, but I did just that. I had on pants and a tee-shirt with my house shoes. While my husband was looking through the mail, I quickly walked down the hall to the bedroom and put on some socks and shoes. I reached in the chest of drawers and pulled out the first pair of socks I could find. At this point, it wasn't about color coordination, it was about speed. I walked out of the bedroom into the hall where we met.

He walked back through my son's bedroom down the four steps into the backyard towards the garage and I followed him. We walked together under the lanai on to the grass. He asked me if I wanted to go into the house. I said, "No! I want to stay with you." The time now was approximately 1:20 p.m.

We walked back into the house as if we were playing follow the leader. We walked through my son's room down the hallway into our bedroom. I went over and sat on the bed while he fumbled with some things on his night stand. I asked him how his day was going and what he had been doing. He reminded me that he stopped by his mother's house and had gotten something to eat, and that earlier he had spoken with his dad.

Then he got up and the walking started all over again. The back door we used to enter and exit from was off my son's bedroom. Outside this door was the backyard. My husband walked down the four steps to go outside again and like before, I followed. Only this time, he turned and walked back up the steps and into the house as if he was going to stay. So, I turned around and walked back up the steps behind him.

As I removed my hand from the door knob, he put his hand on the door knob. I asked him, "What are you doing? Where are you going?" He turned and said to me, "I have to get some toilet tissue out of the garage and take it to the office." I said, "I'll walk back out with you", he replied, "NO! YOU STAY. I HAVE TO GO."

At that moment I really didn't understand the truth and the spiritual meaning or the facts behind his words, "You stay, I have to go."

He opened the door, walked down the four steps to the back yard and into the garage. As I started walking towards the hallway on my way to our bathroom, all of a sudden the Spirit of God inside of me said, "Go to him."

I turned, changing my course and inevitably changing my life path. I stepped fast on my way back through my son's bedroom down the steps to the garage. I wanted to call his name out loud, but I couldn't. Deep in my heart, and remembering the dream, I knew in my heart what was about to happen.

This was between him and God. I stopped about five steps from the garage, and then I heard a gunshot. I tried to push ahead, but I felt a resistance on my chest, as if a hand was holding me back. I even tried stepping to the side, but still, to no use. The Voice of God said, "Wait," so I did.

Not more than a second or two passed and I heard my husband take his last breath as he gave up the ghost, then two seconds later I hear a loud thump. The voice of God said, "Now go."

I looked into the garage and saw my husband slumped over in a chair with his eyes closed. The thump was my husband's gun hitting the concrete floor. I didn't see any blood. It must have been a clean, straight shot through his heart.

Apparently, he sat in the chair, opened his suit jacket and shot himself. All I could say was, "Lord God, You promised never to leave me nor forsake me. Please be with me now." Just as I finished my prayer, I felt God Almighty, Himself, take me by the hand.

I knew not to cry and not to allow my emotions to be released, because I had to stay in control. All at once, fear, rage and pain ran through my mind, but I didn't give in. I knew that Satan's best work is in the realm of our minds and our emotions, and I couldn't give him any place. I started saying, "God! You promised! You promised!"

Instantly, a peace sprang up within me and those negative emotions and feelings subsided. My emotions were still present, but under the influence of the power of God's Peace and Grace, so I pressed forward. I know why my husband chose the garage as the place to take his life. He knew that it was my least favorite space on our property.

Pause!

We lived in a beige with a soft green trim, cottage styled house with a two car garage that needed the door replaced. The garage was cluttered with junk and very disarrayed.

It was disorganized with boxes that were never unpacked and old picture frames from the past owners. It was the place where he knew I would not enter or complain about.

It was all over for my husband. The pain and depression associated with his brother's and his brother's girlfriend's brutal murders, and the secret of his drug addiction were, for him, put to rest. They were no more. But for me, it was just the beginning.

I prayed, "Heavenly Father, give me the strength to go through this and to come out of it victoriously."

I ran into the house and called 911 for the paramedics. I told the operator that my husband shot himself, but instead of suicide, it was reported as a man with a gun.

After hanging up the phone, I ran next door to my neighbor's house, leaving my front door unlocked and wide open. I went next door because my neighbor was a nurse and hopefully she could help. As we ran back to my house, I told her what had happened and where he was.

We ran through my living room, down the hallway, through my son's bedroom and out the back door down the four steps into the yard to the garage where he was. She entered the garage. I ran back into the house to call his dad and his brothers to tell them what had happened. My neighbor and I met in the hallway.

She had a solemn look in her eyes as she reached out her hands to me. I could see in her face my husband was dead. She said, "Go to him."

Now, to the non-believer this might sound cold, but I told her, "No! He's not there." I sincerely needed to believe in my heart that for him, the scripture was true, "For to be absent from the body, is to be present with the Lord" (II CORINTHIANS 5:8).

Minutes later, the police were everywhere. A helicopter was hovering overhead and S.W.A.T. was climbing over the back fence with their guns drawn. By this time, it looked as if the entire LAPD was surrounding my house. With guns pointed at my head and in full gear, the police shouted, "Hands on your head! Hands on your head!"

With their helmets on, the officers looked like Robo-Cops. One officer shouted "Kneel down". I was screaming to them as I knelt down, "My husband shot himself. He's in the garage."

One officer grabbed one of my arms from on top of my head and pulled my hand down behind my back. Then he pulled my other arm down and placed handcuffs on me. He stood me up while another officer pulled back the garage door and went inside to investigate. As the officer exited the garage, he unlatched his helmet and said, "He's dead." With the handcuffs still on me, the officer walked me up the steps through my son's room into my husband's home office.

I sat on the couch and they started rambling through his desk. They were looking for a letter or note or something to corroborate my claim of suicide. Based on their not finding any information, they decided to take me to the police station to test my hands for gunshot residue.

The officer stood me up again, walked me down the hallway through the living room out the front door and to my driveway. At this point, all of my neighbors were out watching and asking what was going on. Cars pulled up. My husband's brothers and his dad jumped out the cars. They ran straight to the house to see what had happened. Obviously, I was not their concern.

By this time, my son was getting out of school. He was attending Loren Miller Elementary School. Remember now, I'm handcuffed, standing in my driveway with a policeman holding a gun on me. When my son turned the corner coming home from school, he saw me and started running towards me. One of the officers drew his weapon on my nine year old son and commanded him to stop. He stopped and started crying, jumping up and down and screaming, "Mommy! Mommy!"

A neighbor came over to console him and to keep him out of harm's way. All I could do to comfort my son, from my position, was to tell him I loved him, and I was all right. Watching my nine year old son screaming in terror about his mother was very painful and overwhelming for me. I was humiliated, embarrassed, disgraced and, from my point of view, misunderstood. The police were like a pack of wolves standing around me waiting for the kill.

Meanwhile, another police officer walked me across the street and forced me into the back seat of a squad car. I watched as complete strangers walked in and out of my home and there was nothing I could do or say about it. Inside my head I could hear voices saying, "Scream! Scream!"

And I wanted to scream, but instead of screaming, I started crying. My crying only lasted for a few seconds when the Spirit of God rose up in me again and I heard God say, "Pray." So I did.

I prayed out loud because I knew that faith comes by hearing. At that point, I needed the God kind of Faith to bring me through this horrible nightmare. I called upon the Name of Jesus Christ reminding God that He had promised never to leave me, nor forsake me (HEBREWS 13:5).

I reminded God of His promise to be with me during the good times and the bad. I reminded God that He is my strong tower, my fortress, my defender and my peace (2 SAMUEL 22:2).

As I ended my prayer, God's peace rose up in me and calmed my spirit. I stopped crying and went into praise. In spite of my current circumstances and those around me, I began to thank God for His love and His mercy and His peace.

I knew God didn't create this dilemma, I also knew, through it all, God was with me. Another officer finally brought my son to me and placed him in the back seat with me. All I could do to comfort my son was lean over, give him a kiss and tell him everything is all right.

At this point, my focus had to stay on the Word of God. I started speaking out loud in the back seat of the squad car words of faith and the Word of God that I could stand on. As I spoke the promises of God's Word, my spirit was energized and my faith was being fortified. Peace and God's love for me was now in control of my emotions. It's true. Whatever is in you will come out (MATTHEW 12:34).

I prayed, "Lord God, in Jesus' Name, hear me now. I will say of the Lord, You are my refuge and my fortress, my God; in You will I trust. A thousand shall fall at my side and ten thousand at my right hand; but it shall not come near me . . . My God, Your grace keeps me and Your peace dwells within me."

I continued to thank God for His comforting Word, His grace and His peace. As I finished the prayer and praise, my son quietly sat up with his shoulders back, and his head lifted with pride. His hearing words of faith gave him strength and faith as well. The officer sitting in the front seat hearing and watching was amazed. I could see it in his face.

After my conversation with God, I could see that the police officer's face was starting to show compassion. The officer stood up, turned facing the squad car as if to take a stretch, then he sat back down facing us with the door open and his legs hanging out. He had a puzzled look on his face.

By this time, I was in control of my emotions and started moving in the authority and the confidence of God. The power of God's Word and my faith produced courage and peace. I asked the officer how long he'd been on the police force. He answered, and somehow a more personal conversation began.

I asked the officer his age and his date of birth and he told me. It was amazing, because his birthday was the same as my now deceased husband's birthday. The officer and my husband were only a year or two apart in age. I could really see in the officer's face that he was thinking about something. My hope was that he was seriously thinking about what I was saying and giving his life to Christ.

I remember now how we started the conversation. While I was sitting in the back seat of the squad car, I almost urinated on myself. The officer told me that it would be against the rules if he permitted me to use the bathroom, because they were going to run a gunshot residue test on my hands for gunpowder.

Once again, it was God's supernatural power working in me. I was able to hold my urine until we reached the police station and have the test done. The test would clear me or convict me of my husband's death.

This was just like Satan. He's the one that steals, kills and destroys. Satan is the one that robs us of life and the goodness of God, and now he was trying to make me out to be a cold-blooded murderer.

15

I was taken to the old 77th Division police station for testing, and if proven guilty, to be booked. At that time, 77th Division had actual human cages for the suspects. Thank God I didn't have to sit in a cage.

They took me directly to the detective's unit. We entered from the back, walked down a hallway, went up some stairs to the next floor, and through a door to the detective's unit. A female police officer read me my Maranda Rights and explained the procedure for the gunshot residue (GSR) test. The test was given first so that I could use the restroom afterwards.

After the test results were known, the detectives were very apologetic and extended sympathy for my loss. They interviewed me again, asking the same questions they had asked earlier. What happened? Where was I when my husband shot himself? What did I do next? All of my answers to everything were the same. My story didn't change. One detective asked me who could they call for my transportation home.

I told them they could call my cousin or my sister. They called my cousin who worked at Good Samaritan Hospital on Wilshire Blvd. The detective told her what had happened and why I had been detained. My cousin told them she would be right there. They permitted me to use the phone and I called my sister. She called my mother and they met us at my home.

When my cousin arrived at 77th Division, they took her aside and asked her about the bullet holes in the office wall of my house. Thinking back on the bullet holes reminded me of how deeply depressed my husband really had been. My cousin told the detectives I was out of town when that happened. I had tried to convince my husband to consider counseling, but his pride would not permit it. Even then, the only thing I knew to do was to pray, so I did!

My cousin drove my son and me home. As we walked up my driveway, on to my front porch into the living room, everything looked the same. However, I knew in my heart that I had to accept the change and prepare to move on with my life.

This was a new chapter in my life and ready or not, I had to embrace it. My consolation was in knowing that God would be with me every step of this journey (PSALM 37:23, 24).

My neighbors came over to see if I was all right and if there was anything they could do to help. My sister offered to stay overnight and I was glad she did. I didn't want to be alone. It was late and I was exhausted.

I don't remember all my family members or neighbors who came to comfort me. However, I do remember my in-laws not being there. All I heard from my deceased husband's family was Just a call from his dad. No one from his family came by to see if I was alive or to grieve with me.

I went to bed before my sister. I laid down on my husband's side of the bed. I needed to be close to him. As I snuggled under the covers, I could smell his body scent in the sheets and that gave me comfort. I tried to imagine his arms around me as I lay thinking, this is real. This is not a dream. Usually, I would wait until my husband got home before I went to sleep. But this night was a new beginning.

As I laid on my left side with my face to the outside, and just as I dosed off, I felt a touch on my cheek. To me, it felt like a kiss. You can believe it or not, but in my heart I knew it was my now deceased husband saying good-by.

Sleeping without him that first night was very difficult. Over the months, we had learned to share a special sleeping routine. He would sleep on his side facing me or with his back to me and I would sleep with my legs draped over him. He would rub my hips like you would sooth a restless baby. That was my first real adjustment to his absence.

I was at a turning point when he first came into my life. Now that he'd left my life, I found myself once again at a turning point. One of his sayings was, "A fair exchange is no robbery". I hope I gave him what God intended for him to have from me.

CHAPTER 2

JEHOVAH TSIDKENU
God my Righteousness
JEREMIAH 23:6

The first morning of my new life began slowly. My first thought was, "He's gone." My second was, "My God, give me your grace to make it through this day and the ability to stand!"

My sister and I got up, had coffee and started making calls to the banks and to my husband's family. Emotions were flaring and hostility was raging by some of my in-laws. My mother, her sister and my aunt's daughter came over to help with the funeral plans.

We found nothing; no insurance policies and very little money in the bank. You see, I trusted our total finances to my husband.

He was the breadwinner and made everything possible and comfortable for my son and me. He paid all the bills and I had no reason not to trust him. Whatever I wanted or needed, he took care of it. I cooked, cleaned and took care of the laundry. He shopped for food, took out the trash, mopped the floors and did what ever else I needed for the family. I did all of my home decor shopping from my home. I became the catalog queen.

I believe God was using my ability to make purchases without physically seeing the items, as a testing ground for trusting

Him. It was truly my beginning in walking by faith and not by sight!

He had been an excellent husband and I do thank God for the time we shared together. In the early months of our relationship and marriage, I felt safe and very secure. Unbeknownst to me, a storm was festering and a plan for enslaving my sanity was being formed.

I'm so glad that God has promised to supply all my need according to His riches in glory through Christ Jesus (PHILIPPIANS 4:19).

My husband died leaving me with a car note, and with lights, gas and insurance payments past due. The mortgage was three months behind and the bank was getting ready to start foreclosure procedures. This is where my Walk of Faith really became reality. I had to make a decision.

My choices were to trust and believe God's Word and live, or to deny God's Word and die. I chose to trust and believe God's Word. I chose to live.

At the time of my husband's suicide, I was a housewife and because of reasons I have not yet explained, I was under a doctor's care. I was totally, financially dependent on my husband. I had no cash money and there was only $115.00 in the bank.

There was no life insurance, because he had let the premiums expire. I discovered my husband had spent $25,000 to $30,000 dollars on cocaine in one year.

This was before crack hit the streets. People would cook the cocaine in order to smoke it. It was called *free basing*. There was nothing free about it. Like the old folks use to say, "The only thing in this life that's free is Jesus."

When we purchased our house, you could buy a three bedroom, two bathroom home in a nice area for $65,000 to $75,000.

Our home was a three bedroom, two bathroom house located two blocks directly behind the old Pepperdine University campus and the new home of Crenshaw Christian Center. This house, like so many other things, was a gift to me from God through my husband.

As a little girl, I never had a doll house, so my husband told me that this house was my adult doll house from him with love. Even after moving out of my doll house, I would dream of returning to it, because I felt I had forgotten something or left something behind.

I didn't have money to bury my husband. His family picked up the cost for his funeral. I thank my Heavenly Father for His Word. The Word of God was all I had to depend on. I only had my faith in God's Word and God's Grace. I held on to the Word of God for dear life.

My husband had a holographic will. He took everything from my son and me and gave it to his father. He took the house, the cars and even gave his half of the car business to his father.

This might sound funny, but at first I put up a fight about the car business. I wanted what rightfully belonged to me. I really wanted to work the car business, but as far as his family was concerned, that was out of the question.

My husband's brother told me to my face I was not going to run his business. I said, "We shall see." Entrepreneurship was in my blood, and with God's Word, I knew I would succeed.

The cousin who drove me home from the police station accompanied me to speak to an attorney regarding the car business and the house. The attorney explained we could fight it, but things would get ugly and he advised me to think it over.

My family and I are from Chicago and we don't believe in sleeping with one eye open. In other words, where I come from, we believe not only should Satan be under your feet, but your earthly enemy should be under your feet as well.

I decided this battle wasn't worth it. My peace of mind was worth much more than what money could buy. I knew in my heart God had something better for me. Entrepreneurship was my future, but not in cars.

I released the car business and my husband's Mercedes to my in-laws. My father-in-law spoke up and insisted the house and the powder blue Cadillac Seville belonged to me. Everyone knew that the Cadillac was a birthday gift from my deceased husband. However, it would be my decision to keep them or give them up. I decided to keep them. From the business, all I wanted was the furniture in my husband's office at the car lot. His brother agreed.

I was able to pick up the two burgundy, Queen Ann chairs with ottomans, the side table and a magazine table. I had to leave behind his beautiful desk with matching cabinet and a swivel, high back chair.

I made arrangements to pick the remaining furniture up the next day. On the next day, when I arrived at the car lot, I found the furniture outdoors in the parking lot, chopped up. That beautiful furniture looked like someone took an ax and chopped everything for firewood. Tears rose up in my eyes. It boggles my mind to think they hated me that much or blamed me for something I had no control over.

I tried to warn his family something was wrong with my husband, but no one really listened. Like the incident with the bullet holes. I had gone out of town to visit my aunt in Chicago. This aunt was my father's oldest sister and she was recovering from breast cancer surgery. My grandmother told my sister and me we should go visit our aunt while she could appreciate and enjoy the visit.

Because of his drug abuse, my husband was so insecure and paranoid, he believed my reason for going on this trip was just an excuse to leave him. He believed if I left, I would not come back. To prove I was coming back, I allowed my son to stay with him. My sister and I departed Christmas night and planned to return three days later.

Instead of staying with my aunt, my sister and I stayed with our father's oldest daughter. She lived with her mother, who happened to be my father's third wife. They lived in a beautiful home outside of Chicago. My dad married her mother and adopted her when she was two years old. I loved my dad's third wife because she truly had God's love in her heart. She always gave me a mother's love. During our visit, we had fun doing the things a mother would do with her daughters.

You see, I was the first of the many of my father's bastard children he claimed. I was the hook my mother used to get and keep my father's attention. Daddy would always say it was her beauty that hooked him, but it was me that kept him around.

I was just like the stick when a child is finished eating ice cream off of it. The stick is sucked and chewed until all the ice cream is gone and then the stick is thrown away. The stick has no future use.

While growing up, that's the way I felt, used and unwanted! As the story goes, my mother was a virgin and that's the only reason I was claimed as a Thompson. And whenever my Daddy had a drink or two, he made it known.

Now back to my Chicago trip. The confusion started the third day of our trip. My husband called me long distance just one day

23

before we were scheduled to return home and told me that he was going to kill himself.

He was not loud or out of control. He spoke with a soft voice at first, but as our conversation progressed, his tone grew louder and louder. I assured him of my love and that I would take an early flight home if necessary. He agreed to calm down and told me he was just missing me.

In a silent state of panic, I hung up the phone and called his dad. I pleaded for him to call and go see what was going on because my son was there. His dad called and talked to my husband and called me back. He tried to convince me everything was fine and not to worry, but in my spirit, I knew better.

I prayed, "God, please keep my son safe." If my husband's intention was to ruin my trip, he succeeded. That last night I had to take a drink to calm my nerves and, I prayed myself to sleep.

When I got home, and saw the holes in the wall, I asked my son what had happened. He told me his step-father went for pizza and left him for hours by himself. He went on to say when his step-father returned, the pizza was cold and he was acting strange.

My son told me his step-father had walked around the house with a loaded gun trying to decide if he was going to kill himself or not. Instead of shooting himself, he shot twice into the mirrored closet door of his office. That's how the bullet holes got there. The bullets went through the closet door and the clothes hanging up in the closet and came out on the other side into the next room.

My son told me he ran into his room and pushed his solid, maplewood, skipper style twin bed from the wall in his room, and slid down behind it. He hid under his bed for safety. His bed was three feet off the floor with two drawers underneath and book selves on each end. The bed was heavy and hard for an adult to move, so imagine the fear in my son that motivated him to move his bed. I promised my son I would never leave him like that again. Never!

Pause!

The evening when we viewed the body was a nightmare. The atmosphere was like two rival sports teams out to kill each other. His family was on one side of the room and my family on the other.

My family went in first to view the body because I was the wife. I don't remember his mother or father wanting to go in with me to view his body. The mortuary didn't care about the anger or the conflict. Their only concern was to do what was right.

There were light cuts on my husband's neck from the mortuary shaving him. The rumors were that my husband and I fought before his death and the cuts were from my fingernails. My husband's family didn't understand that all they were doing was giving place to the devil, and my family was thinking, "If you feel like a frog, jump froggy jump." The Word of God tells us to put on the whole armor of God so we will be able to stand in the evil day (EPHESIANS 6:11).

Well, my blood family did it literally. The next time the families met, my family was armed and dangerous. My deceased husband loved my grandmother and she loved him. In spite of her love for him, she wasn't going to tolerate his family's disrespect towards her or her granddaughter. She carried with her the most power of all. She carried God's Word in her heart and a friend in her purse. I hope you get my drift.

The day of my husband's memorial service was a test of walking in love. Early that morning, I read PSALM 23: *The Lord is my shepherd; I shall not want. He maketh me to lie down in green pastures: He leadeth me beside the still waters. He restoreth my soul: He leadeth me in the paths of righteousness for His Name's sake. Yea, though I walk through the valley of the shadow of death, I will fear no evil: for Thou art with me; Thy rod and Thy staff they comfort me. Thou preparest a table before me in the presence of mine enemies: Thou anointest my head with oil; my cup runneth over. Surely goodness and mercy shall follow me all the days of my life: and I will dwell in the house of the Lord for ever.*

I also read PSALM 25: 1-5: *Unto Thee, O Lord, do I lift up my soul. O my God, I trust in Thee: let me not be ashamed, let not mine enemies triumph over me. Yea, let none that wait on Thee be ashamed: let them be ashamed which transgress without cause. Shew me Thy ways, O Lord; teach me Thy paths. Lead me in Thy truth, and teach me: for thou art the God of my salvation; on Thee do I wait all the day.*

After that, I read PSALM 27: 1-3, 14: *The Lord is my light and my salvation; whom shall I fear? the Lord is the strength of my life; of whom shall I be afraid? When the wicked, even mine enemies and my foes, came upon me to eat up my flesh, they stumbled and fell. Though an host should encamp against me, my heart shall not fear: though war should rise against me, in this will I be confident. Wait on the Lord: be of good courage, and He shall strengthen thine heart: wait, I say, on the Lord.*

My deceased husband's family was so cold-hearted towards me. They acted as if I had pulled the trigger myself. Satan had succeeded in making me look like a cold-blooded murderer and all I tried to do was stand by my man.

I loved him physically and mentally. I prayed with him and for him. I was there to cheer him on in his successes and encourage him at his lowest points in business, but the seduction and influences of the drugs were greater.

The saddest part about his memorial was there was no communication between the two households regarding the transportation or the repast. The division was so great that our families even had separate limousine cars. One car went to my husband's parents' house and another came to my house. He had a lot of friends and family attending the service, which was held at

Angeles Funeral Home, and he was buried at Inglewood Park Cemetery. Without my consent, opinion, or approval, the repast was held at his parent's home. Our limousine was instructed to drop us off at my house. The funeral home attendants opened the car doors and we got out.

Silently, we all walked up the driveway to the front porch and stepped into the house. We talked among ourselves and I decided we should go to my in-laws for the repast, anyway. I pleaded my case with my family, because I was determined to walk in God's Love, no matter how they treated me. So, my family agreed to go. There were eight of us, which meant we had to take two cars.

When we walked through the front door, you could feel the tension and see the hate in their eyes. As the old folks would say, if eyes could cut, we would be dead. My sister-in-law's sister was the only one who extended hospitality toward me and my family. We accepted the kindness and showed gratitude.

She offered my family and me something to eat and she served me with a heart of compassion. I was hoping that this would be my last experience of evil and ugliness from my in-laws, but unfortunately, there was more to come.

CHAPTER 3

JEHOVAH JIREH
God is my Provider
GENESIS 22:14

$\mathcal{N}$o one in my deceased husband's family, or even in my family intended to help me save my house. I turned to Jesus and began to really search the scriptures for an answer. God's Word said, "Ask, seek and knock so I did (LUKE 11:9).

After the memorial service, my neighbors gathered around me with more than just words. From them, more than $500.00 cash was given to me. The amazing part was I hadn't said anything to anyone about my financial state.

That was my Heavenly Father taking care of me. God knew my need before I even asked. Praises be to God! Everybody was telling me what I should do, but no one was saying what I could do, or how to do it.

Like I said before, I lived right around the corner from the old Pepperdine University campus, the future home of Crenshaw Christian Center. My husband and I purchased the house two months prior to Crenshaw buying Pepperdine's property.

My husband had always been against my attending Sunday worship services and mid-week day or night Bible Study. Going to Crenshaw Christian Center was out of the question. He used the large crowds and difficult parking situations as an excuse. But, thanks be to God for Christian television.

I watched Dr. Fredrick K. C. Price on Ever Increasing Faith twice a week and Herbert W. Armstrong and Kenneth Copeland just to name a few. But most of all, I had the Spirit of God. The Holy Spirit! That was my real teacher.

As I stated before, during my marriage, my husband didn't want me to go to church, so to keep peace, I didn't go. I would spend hours in the chair in my bedroom reading and studying my Bible. I studied the book of Revelations because I wanted to know the end and how we win.

To me, it was surely a blessing. My church was within walking distance of my home. I thought to myself, "No more parking problems for me."

However, after my husband's death, Satan was doing everything in his power to get me put out of my house and away from Crenshaw Christian Center.

After the confusion with my in-laws about the house, I asked God what He wanted me to do to sustain it. I was comfortable and I didn't want to move, but I clearly understood, *not my will Lord; but Your will be done in my life.*

I knew that my home was a gift to me from my Heavenly Father through my husband. On our very first visit to see the house, the owners embraced us and eagerly stated they were hoping a loving, young couple would purchase the house and make it a home.

The previous owners were an older Christian, Caucasian couple who had lived in that house for over thirty years. The whole house had a pleasant feeling. The back yard, with its beautiful rose bushes and birds of paradise, were to me, a little piece of heaven on earth.

Prior to my husband's death, I had spent many, many hours praying in the backyard, praising and thanking God for His goodness and His mercy. Little did I know my backyard would continue to be a place of God's Presence, and a sanctuary for me to study God's Word; to praise God in dance and to listen for God's instructions during such perilous times.

After my husband's death, my study time in God's Word became intensified. Now, I was able to attend Monday, Tuesday and Friday night Bible Studies. I was now in the School of the Holy Spirit.

At that time, I didn't realize I had begun a fast and consecration that would set the course for the things to come. When my son was in school, I would pray and read my Bible and other Word inspired materials. At that time, I didn't understand, but today I know I was hearing the Voice of God behind the written Word. I was being taught by the Spirit of the Most High God.

The only person I would talk to about spiritual things was my grandmother. My grandmother was Baptist and she was rooted in the Baptist tradition, but she was the only other person in my life who could possibly understand where my walk with Christ was headed.

She would watch Ever Increasing Faith on television on Friday evenings and on Sunday mornings whenever she didn't attend her church. There is one spiritual truth my grandmother instilled in me and I will carry it into eternity. She would tell me, "God's Grace is sufficient." And I would ask her, "Mama, what do you mean?" She would say again, "God's Grace is sufficient" (II CORINTHIANS 12:9-10).

Pause!

One night I walked outside and stood in the front of my house, looked up to the heavens and, with determination in my heart, I declared, "He that is in me is greater than he that is in the world" (1JOHN 4:4). Then I called upon the Greater One that indwells me. I asked God for knowledge, wisdom, and a way to keep my house. I was not eligible for S.S.I., welfare or unemployment. The only benefit I was eligible for was my deceased husband's Social Security which was $334.00 a month; just enough to pay my car note.

Looking back, I'm glad I had no safety net to catch me or to keep me from falling. All I had was the Word of God. God's Word says to "stand" and that's exactly what I did (EPHESIANS 6:13-14).

An example that I will never forget is this. I was sitting in my backyard studying my Bible and I had a taste for fried chicken.

About two hours after my thought, my neighbor's brother, the neighborhood drunk, came over to see how I was doing. He told me God told him I wanted some fried chicken. He just wanted to know what brand of chicken I would like. This might seem unimportant or trivial, but it's when the heart's desires are being fulfilled that makes walking with God so sweet. To me, that was just one of God's little kisses.

I had to literally live by faith and ignore my circumstances and my emotions. The good thing about this foundational lesson in faith is that it has empowered me to succeed in everything I put my hands to. I was embarking on the Revelation of God and getting ready to experience the Grace of God that my grandmother was talking about. We serve an awesome God.

Chapter 4

Jehovah M'Kaddesh
My God Sanctifies
Leviticus 20:7-8

I enjoyed staying at home. Keeping that in mind, I thought and prayed "God, I've trusted you in the past and I trust You now. Tell me what I can do, that would allow me to stay home, but still make money." God said, "Children!"

After making some phone calls, I looked into foster care. The state requires additional income before you can apply, so for me, foster care was out. I looked into home day care.

I applied for a home day care license and of course, Satan and his demon crowd did everything they could to try to slow me down and stop the process. However, to God be the glory! I used every stumbling block as a stepping stone.

My license was approved and granted on the first home visit and it was issued July 2, 1982. According to California State Law, I could keep no more than six children at a time. Therefore, in order to meet my mortgage payments and other living expenses, I had to do something different. God gave me the idea to offer child care services for non-traditional hours.

That meant earlier hours, later hours and weekends. I had children twenty-four hours a day, seven days a week. I would eat when the children ate and sleep when they slept. Children became my life. The children in my care went with me to Children's Church on Sundays and on Fridays to Friday night Bible Study. Many of the parents were happy to have their children with me and to know that their children were in a Christian environment. The parents recognized and appreciated the positive influences of God's Word in their children's lives.

Let me tell you how walking in the sanctification of Jesus Christ and having a pure heart to serve Almighty God will ignite the supernatural power of God in our lives.

I had a little girl in my care about three years old. She was happy with a great personality. One sunny, summer morning after breakfast I took the children outdoors for class and playtime. What I didn't know was this little girl had a history of seizures.

She was running and playing like the other children. She walked up to me and as I went to pick her up, she collapsed in my arms. This was before first-aid and CPR training was a requirement, and don't forget her mother didn't tell me that she had seizures. I picked her up and ran across the street to my neighbor's house.

My neighbor worked in a hospital, but she was not a nurse. We laid the little girl down on the kitchen floor. When I realized that my neighbor didn't know what to do, I did what I knew to do! I laid my hands on the little girl and commanded that she be healed in the Name of Jesus.

Then I went into praise and thanked God for healing her. Within a minute, she took a deep breath. My neighbor just looked at me with a puzzled expression on her face. I picked up the little girl and she gave me a hug. I thanked my neighbor for her help and walked back across the street to my house. The little girl was fine. She never had another seizure while in my care.

You see God is true and faithful to His Word. We can trust God in everything.

Pause!

I made up my mind I was going to tithe. Regardless of whatever my financial situation was, I was going to tithe. The phone and gas company might only get half, but God was going to get all of His. And praise God, not only did I tithe, but I began to give into the gospel.

Every Bible Study I attended, I gave into the offering. I could only give five dollars in the offering, but it all adds up. I also gave to Trinity Broadcasting Network (TBN). Tithing opens the windows of Heaven for the blessings, but giving determines the amount of the return blessing (II CORINTHIANS 9:6; GALATIANS 6:7). So please don't be cheap in your giving!

I attended Monday, Tuesday and Friday night Bible Studies. That's fifteen dollars a week times four weeks, that's sixty dollars or more a month, plus I was giving into other ministries.

I knew God's Word works and I expected my return on my giving. What did I have to lose? God's Word promised the windows of heaven blessing and God said He would rebuke the devil when you tithe. I wanted everything God had for me.

My suggestion to anyone who is in doubt about tithing is, become a tither and you will see what a Mighty God we serve (MALACHI 3: 10-11). After all, God tells us to prove Him.

I placed an ad in the Los Angeles Sentinel newspaper and passed out flyers everywhere I went. In the first week I had three children. The next week I received another child and the following week, two more came. By the end of the month, I had six children. Praise God! The money was coming in, but so was Satan.

A past due property tax notice came in the mail. But, I saw it as another opportunity to trust God, and as promised, God supplied the need.

My father-in-law informed me I had a few years before this debt had to be settled. Thank You, Jesus! Not one cent of my hard earned money went towards paying the back taxes. I moved out of the house before the debt had to be paid.

Pause!

In the summer of 1979, I had just graduated from Los Angeles Trade Technical College with an Associate of Arts Degree and was two months into the new semester at my new school.

I was a full time student at the University of Southern California majoring in psychology. I was not yet finished with my education and I had no job, but God was in my life, and God held my future.

Early childhood education was not my area of study, but when God directs, God always provides (I Corinthians 2:9; Ephesians 3:20). All I knew was my upbringing. I had a son and I had younger cousins I took care of in the past, so I had some understanding of the needs of children, but no bona fide training.

About six months into the business, God brought a grandmother with her one year old grandson to my door for child care. I interviewed the grandmother and her daughter. They were pleased with my home and with what I had to offer.

Not only did she utilize my services, but she was a pre-school teacher with the Head Start program as well as a Christian and a member of Crenshaw Christian Center.

She had completed training in the High Scope Early Childhood Education Curriculum and was preparing to become a head teacher and trainer of it. God had every thing in place for me. She became one of my mentors and a close friend.

We are still friends to this day. During those financially trying times of the Reagan Rule, when he cut California budgets drastically, she would bring my child care milk, eggs, cheese and beans. She would donate crayons, paper and seasonal art projects to my child care for the children to use.

I put my faith in God and God's promises, and things have always worked out for my best. *Trust in the Lord with all your heart, and lean not on your own understanding; in all your ways acknowledge Him, and He shall direct your paths* (PROVERBS 3:5-6).

During the next year and a half I experienced real Christian maturing. I was still in school. It wasn't USC. It was the School of the Holy Spirit and I was going to ace all of my classes.

With God, it's pass or repeat. You will repeat the classes until you get it right. There's no age limit, color preference, or height requirement, just faith. Without faith, it's impossible to please God (HEBREWS 11:6). Today, I don't just believe it, I KNOW IT.

At this point in my walk with God, my classes were on fear and death and what I call simple faith. An example of my overcoming fear was through a dream I had.

Back in Chicago, when I was about four or five years old, my dress caught on fire. I had climbed up on a chair to get something off the stove. I reached over to the back burner not knowing that the front burner was on low. My dress caught on fire. I screamed and my aunt heard me. She ran in and grabbed me and threw me on the bed to put out the fire. Every since then, I had a fear of fire (II TIMOTHY 1:7).

Keeping that in mind, Satan put me to a test. My question was; what was being tested? Was the test on my fear of burning to death or the fear of death itself? One night, while I was asleep, I started dreaming that I was on fire and burning. I could feel my flesh burning and I couldn't move. I heard Satan say, "You are going to die."

I thought, "To be absent from the body is to be present with the Lord" (2 CORINTHIANS 5:8). I thought, "Lord I'm coming!" And the dream ended. I woke up and that was that. I now have no fear of fire or of dying.

At the end of my day and when the doors were all locked, I would tell my angels to stand watch over me and my household and I would pray and thank God for that night's sweet sleep. I would close my eyes and go to sleep. I trusted God, not only to keep me and my son safe, but also my possessions (PROVERBS 3: 24).

For me, now, death is just the door to my Jesus, and my eternity. Today, I respect fire and its ability, but without fear.

Simple faith was not looking to my clients as my source, but to God. When a client would leave for whatever the reason, I had to trust God as my Provider to send another one.

Things were tight, but my needs were always met. My lights, gas and phone were never turned off and there was always food to eat. Those days were foundational and priceless. God is truly Jehovah Jireh – My Provider. I am sanctified by God through Jesus Christ.

Chapter 5

Jehovah Shammah
The Ever Present One
Ezekiel 48:35

*I*n 1979, as a pedestrian, I was hit by a car. I was drug under the car approximately 150 feet. The only reason the driver stopped was because he drove into a parked car. But, praise God, I am here to tell you about it.

Not only was I hit and drug under the car, but the doctors said, because of the injuries I sustained, I must have turned over under the car. Praise God for His mercy! Not one bone in my body was broken.

I suffered first and third degree burns over my entire body. Burns were on my back, breasts, elbows, knees, ankles, fingers, hands and forehead. Cuts were everywhere, but the worst was yet to come.

My left hip was totally dislocated, and on my left leg I had a third degree burn starting from my buttocks down the back of the thigh. My body had been pinned under the car and my left thigh was wedged by the car's muffler which caused the burn.

The burn reached around to my knee to a depth just above the muscle. The doctors said that I was lucky, but I know better. It was God's mercy on my life. My hip was put back in place without surgery. The depth and the size of the burn required a skin graft.

The nerves in the right side of my face were numb. I could barely open my mouth or use my peripheral vision. In order to see on either side, I had to turn my whole head. I was swollen, both my eyes were black, and I couldn't sit up. My entire body was in a state of shock. I was unconscious for three days. They told my family and friends I could have brain damage.

Meanwhile, everybody prayed and waited. After I woke up, I remember my friends coming to visit me and I could see the horrified expression on their faces. I looked just that bad.

To add another dimension to my testimony, my own father was in another hospital, dying of cancer, and here it looked like I was about to beat him to the grave. But praise God, I lived to be able to tell this story.

When I regained consciousness and opened my eyes, my room was filled with flowers, cards and gifts. My son's classmates made individual get-well cards and they were posted on the wall above my head.

I had every type of flower arrangement sold in the hospital's gift shop. It made me feel good to know that many people loved and cared about me.

This was the beginning of the demonstration of the influence God would have on people and their lives through my life and my confession of Jesus the Christ (JOHN 12:32).

When I finally came to myself, my family had to tell me what had happened. I had no remembrance of anything at all. I spent three weeks in the hospital and I had to use a urinary catheter during my first week and a half.

My digestive system and my process of elimination had to re-adjust along with the rest of my body. Therefore, for a while, I was fed intravenously. I was re-introduced to solid foods slowly. Of course, my menstrual cycle shut down. It took two months for my hormones to regulate. I was hit so hard, blood was in my urine, and of course, that meant more tests and medications.

In the hospital, it seems the nurses are not concerned about the patient's looks or fashion. After three days of being in the hospital, my hair was still full of glass, oil and dirt from my head being drug on the asphalt. And because of the head injury, neither the nurses nor my family were allowed to clean or even brush my hair. I had to be completely conscious before anyone could touch my head. So you can imagine what I looked like.

I remember trying to recall my life. It was a very slow, one thing at a time process. First, I thought, I'm in school. I attend USC. I have a six year old son. God is true to His Word.

The Holy Spirit promises to bring all things to our remembrances, while at the same time, God is our shield and our fortress. My circumstance said I should be dead! But thanks be to God, He said, "Live."

Praise God! God removed the total ordeal from my memory. I didn't remember being hit, drug, or anything. Even to this day, I still don't remember. To God be the glory for the marvelous things He has done for me (PROVERBS 3: 25-26)!

After I became stable, a skin graft was performed on my left thigh. The first skin graft did not take and gangrene set in. The graft site became infected because the bandages needed to be changed three times daily, but they weren't.

At one point, the thought was to amputate. But praise God, prayer works. The old skin had to be removed so a second skin graft could be performed.

It was the hospital's negligence that caused the gangrene, but the thought of suing the hospital wasn't on my mind. I didn't understand until much later what had really caused the first skin graft to get infected. The nurses had been negligent.

But the extra drama of needing a second skin graft and believing God just added to my developing faith. The hospital permitted me to go home and have private duty nursing care. I was at home for three weeks before the second skin graft was performed. My cousin, the same one who picked me up from the police station, was my private duty nurse.

Pause!

My son and I lived in a two bedroom, two story, upstairs apartment next to the 110 freeway. I had four windows in the entire apartment. One window was in the living room, one in the dining area, and one in each of the bedrooms. The only windows that opened were the ones in the living room and the bedrooms. The kitchen was open and attached to the dining area. The bathroom was upstairs with a vent.

My family decided I needed a hospital bed and other equipment, so my living room became my sleeping place and my place of recovery. I had to hop on one leg up the stairs to take a shower then hop back down to go to sleep.

What I enjoyed most about this apartment was, when I looked out of the windows, all I would see was tall trees in the summer and blue skies in fall. So, I would imagine I was in a forest or on a hilltop. I would sit up in the bed looking at the wheelchair and say to it, "I will never need you, because I have Jesus."

Each time my cousin would change the bandage, she could see new skin appearing. The new growth allowed the necrotic or dead skin from the failed graft to drop off and be washed away. Praise God! I was getting better and at the same time my faith was growing.

I was determined to get up from my home hospital bed and do for myself. My plans were to not only walk again, but I was going to dance again as well.

I enjoyed dancing! Dancing was more than entertainment and fun for me. My dancing was expressive, creative and seductive. In the world, the seductiveness would work in my favor but not in the body of Christ. God changed the seductiveness to an anointing! As with everything else, God was ordering my steps (PSALMS 30:10-12).

47

I was able to watch the Ever Increasing Faith broadcasts on Friday evenings and Sunday mornings along with other Christian television ministries. I would have my own Bible study, just me and the Holy Spirit. At this point in my life, I had no outside influences or distractions.

My grandmother told me, "God has you where He wants you." And now I understood what she was saying. We both knew God didn't cause the accident, but because of my ungodly choices and the worldly decisions I had made, God permitted it to happen. I had placed myself in an environment of selfishness and indulgence and Satan seized the opportunity to try and take my life.

I recognize now God had a destiny and purpose for my life. You can bet from that point on, God had my full attention. ROMANS 6:23 says: *For the wages of sin is death, but the gift of God is eternal life in Christ Jesus our Lord.*

Let's take a little side-bar for a moment. Before the accident occurred, even though I had made a commitment to serve God through Jesus Christ, old habits were still in control. In the summer prior to the accident, I realized a hardening of my heart was setting in.

I would not consider myself as sleeping around. To me, sleeping around implies spending time with someone, and that's not what I was doing. I would hit it and quit it.

At first, in order for me to have sex with someone, there had to be an attraction. I had a full tuition scholarship from U.S.C. and I was still eligible for my student loans. I had a plan. But because of sin, I was becoming heartless. By the end of that summer, it was on.

It was becoming very easy for me to have sexual intercourse with men and feel nothing toward them. I would have sexual intercourse in exchange for material things such as clothing and jewelry or whatever I needed for my son and me.

By the second week of the new semester, one of my professors was calling me at my home and another professor on campus was desperately trying to get my attention. Yes, I had a plan, but "thank you sweet Jesus!"

Even though it hurt my body, I'm truly thankful God had His plan for my life. I need you to understand GOD DID NOT CAUSE the accident. It was my ungodly decisions that opened the door for the accident to happen. Let me explain ungodly decisions.

One of my long time girlfriends stopped by my apartment to tell me something tragic would happen if I went out that up coming Halloween weekend. At first I took her seriously. I told my date, who was my special friend, what she said, and I was thinking about not going out with him.

He said very casually, "O. K." and added that he would ask one of his old girlfriends to spend the weekend with him. Of course, you know my pride and flesh would not stand for that.

The idea of another woman being with him was out of the question! He really wanted me to go with him and he knew what would get under my skin and make me jealous. I ignored the warning and committed to go with him anyway. The rest is history.

Pause!

Now let's get back to where I left off about my recovery from the accident. I would read my Bible and meditate on God's Word all day. My sleep pattern was unusual also. I would wake-up around 5:30 a.m., take a nap about 11:00 a.m., and be asleep for the night by 7:30 p.m. God would wake me up sometimes around 1:00 a.m. and I would pray. This prayer schedule was the beginning of a prayer pattern that exists to this day.

After the three weeks of home recuperation were up, I returned to the hospital for the second skin graft. My hospital stay this time was a week. The second graft was successful and I had over 50 small stitches to hold the new skin in place. I had to hold my left leg straight and not bend it.

If I bent my leg, it would cause the muscle to flex which in turn would burst the stitches. And that would greatly interfere with the healing process. I was able to keep my leg straight and therefore I had no keloid and no infection.

Whenever I stood and stepped, my right side had to support the weight of my entire body. As a result of my hip injury and the resetting of the hip, the tendons and muscles connecting and those between the ball and socket of my hip had a heavy calcium deposit and the calcium was increasing. My doctor said I would probably need my hip joint replaced by the time I was thirty-five.

I subsequently had the hip replacement, but that's another testimony of God's healing provision. Also, my left leg was at least two inches shorter than the right leg, so I walked with a limp. I had to learn how to balance and walk again.

It was over fifteen weeks after the accident before I could put my left foot on the floor to walk. My physical therapist was the Holy Spirit. The doctors said I would never dance again because the pressure on the hip, as well as the pain, would be too much to bear.

As I previously stated, before the accident, dancing was more then entertainment for me. I would contract to dance for special functions and events at school and in the community. I enjoyed creative dancing and it kept me in good physical shape.

I must confess and tell the truth that all during this period of my life, I smoked marijuana. I smoked marijuana in order to stay in a totally relaxed state of mind. The marijuana was my medication.

After my son went to school in the morning, my rehabilitation routine was prayer and praise. Then I would smoke a marijuana cigarette, turn the music on and get a good workout. I would stretch and bend to tone the muscles that supported my hip.

I realized that smoking marijuana was wrong, but at that point in my life, it was helping me make it through. The medication the doctors prescribed for me was too strong and caused hallucinations.

I told my doctor about the home grown marijuana and he gave me the okay to smoke in lieu of the medication. My doctor also told me if I couldn't get any marijuana on my own, I could get a prescription.

The herb was used so I would be able to relax, and stretch and strengthen my body, but it was not used for the pain. I thank God that He deals with us at our own individual personal levels (HEBREWS 12:1).

My hip had some rotation in it, but the circulation in my left leg was not working so well. I could only walk for about half a block without having a pain attack. Bending over quickly was painful. And as I said before, I didn't like the effect the medications had on me.

I was not a drinker, but I had to deal with the pain some way. My hip injury was too new, and I was too young to have the hip surgery. The doctors told me I should try to endure the pain. So I did the best I could.

CHAPTER 6

Jehovah Nissi
God Fights My Battle
Exodus 17:15

Going back even further, it was the mid 70s when I decided to further my education, so I enrolled in a community college. But, even before that, I was employed by the County of Los Angeles Superior Courts Division and my site was in the heart of downtown LA.

One of my co-workers was reading a book entitled *How Faith Works*, written by Pastor Fred Price. After she finished it, she let me read the book. The book opened my eyes to the reality of a guaranteed successful, godly life. When she saw I was interested, she started sharing with me about the Monday night Bible Studies and the church she attended which happened to be Crenshaw Christian Center.

She extended an invitation to me and I accepted. Not only did I attend on Monday nights, but whenever I could get a ride, I would attend Sunday morning services.

The teaching was something I had never heard before. This teaching could be applied and utilized in a person's everyday life. The taste of God's Word took hold of my spirit and I wanted more, but that's when the war began.

During this time of my life, I was frustrated and very unhappy. I was truly between a rock and a hard place. I had broken up with my first true love and I was in a dead-end job and wanted more out of life.

That's when I realized in order to advance with the County of Los Angeles I needed to further my education. For me, that meant becoming a full-time student. It sounded like a good idea, but as far as my father and other members of my family were concerned, I was out of my cotton-picking mind.

My father was outraged at me for even thinking about quitting my civil service job. He even threatened not to help me if things got financially tight. My father was so disappointed with me he stopped speaking to me for a while, but that didn't last long. The silence only lasted about two weeks, because I was a daddy's girl.

I'm even named after my father. In order to keep his lineage alive, he refused to give me a middle name. His thinking was, when I married, I would use my maiden name as a middle name. All my life I heard, "You are a Thompson, and you will always be a Thompson." It worked. Faith does come by hearing! Check out my name.

Before my father's death, I had the opportunity and privilege to grace him with a demonstration of my achievements. In my last semester at Los Angeles Trade-Technical College, my father attended our Black History Celebration.

I was the Mistress of Ceremony and was scheduled to perform. Just before I danced at the celebration, I was able to introduce my father to the audience.

My father was sitting on the front row with my son. My father, who was a big, tall man, stood up, turned to the audience and waved. As he sat down, the applause began. The clapping and cheering grew and continued until the audience started standing. Everyone in the auditorium was on their feet clapping and cheering. My daddy received a standing ovation. He was honored for being my father and I was so proud to be his daughter!

Pause!

What I'm about to say is very difficult for me. But as I previously stated, before the accident I was not walking in the fullness of God's Word. Even though God was moving in my life and had granted me a full tuition scholarship to USC, I was still doing things my way.

I didn't have the revelation or understanding of fornication and the impact of it on my spirit and my relationship with God (I CORINTHIANS 3:16; 6:13; 6:15-20).

Sex outside of marriage was a way of life for me. Sometimes sex was a means to an end, but mainly in my life, I used sex as the method of searching for fulfillment. I was searching for love and fulfillment in men and still not being satisfied.

What I was searching and looking for could only be found in God, through Jesus Christ. So if you are walking down this road, STOP! You PAUSE! GO READ (ROMANS 10: 9-10).

Pause!

I need to give a little history here. During my junior and senior high school years, I was blessed to grow up in a middle class neighborhood where I saw healthy marriage relationships.

As a teen-ager, even though my own family was dysfunctional, I witnessed husbands and wives working together for a common goal, which was the family.

Even as a young child and living in the projects of Aliso Village in East Los Angeles, and in spite of the poor economic conditions and other circumstances, I still saw healthy marriages.

However, I also saw in the projects, women being used by men, and children being neglected. So I had a good understanding of both kinds of relationships. I witnessed what a good relationship looked like and what a one-sided relationship looked like as well.

My mother was an alcoholic, so my siblings and I were tossed back and forth between my father, his sister and mother. My mother lived in the projects and in the late 60s she was on the wagon while we were living with her.

After I graduated from elementary school, my father bought the house next door to his sister and her husband and moved all of us in. I saw my own father going to work come hell or high water, sick or well, because he had a family to feed. I thank God for my uncle, because at that time in my life he was the only example I had of a godly man.

As adults, my sister and I asked our father why he didn't get sole custody of us. My father's answer was that he didn't want us to ever say he took us from our mother. My sister and I looked at each other and I told daddy, "You would have done us a favor."

My father dropped his head. My sister and I gave him a big hug and told him we were fine, because he was always there.

One thing I'm sure of is having a good relationship with my earthly father made it easy for me to embrace God's plan for salvation through Jesus the Christ and God's unconditional love for my life (JOHN 3:16-17).

I would say to any one who has never experienced a natural love of a father not to fear (I PETER 2:9). God's love is pure, protecting and eternal. Know this; regardless of your past, God's Word will secure your future (PSALM 37:18-19).

Pause!

My parents moved us to California in August of 1960. We first lived with my father's middle sister and her husband. Later, we moved next door to them. My aunt and uncle were foster parents and they housed teenage boys.

Well, it's true what they say about abused children having the potential to become abusers. I was six years old when one of the teenage boys tricked me into going into the outdoor wash house. He unzipped his zipper and put his penis in my mouth and told me to suck it. He told me if I didn't do it I would get in trouble. After he was satisfied he continued to threaten me by saying if I told, he would hurt me.

Before our coming to California, I was protected by my father. I was pure and totally innocent. Now, in California my father worked away from home four days out of a week. This incident took place during his absence.

My father went to his grave never knowing what had happen to his little girl. I don't remember how long it took or when it happened, but God suppressed the memory of the sexual molestation and everything associated with this event from my mind, and I'm glad He did.

However, in my teenage years, when I became sexually active, the erotic thoughts surfaced as promiscuity. I enjoyed giving and receiving oral sex. The secret of the actual sexual molestation was deeply hidden and the long term effect didn't completely surface until years later into my future marriage. As a result of the flashback, it was mentally difficult for me to kiss and freely love my husband.

Let me explain the flashback. While watching a television talk show, the topic happened to be incest and its effect on children and their behavior into adulthood. As I sat on the edge of my bed, watching and listening to the program, the memory of the teenager's penis in my mouth flashed before me. All of a sudden I felt devastated, embarrassed, and frightened! I started crying, and for a moment, I felt so alone. It took several months for these feelings of fear to subside. But praises be to God, in my tears, the cleaning and healing began.

As I studied God's Word, the fear and embarrassment of the sexual molestation began to fade away. You see, what is done in the dark will eventually come to the light, be it good or bad.

Even in one of my darkest moments, God's uncompromising love pierced through and cut out the pain and humiliation. As I replaced the ungodly thoughts of Satan's voice with God's Word, I regained confidence and self-worth in what God says about me.

It doesn't matter what has happen in your life. Just know, God's Love will heal it all. Do what I did, and that is, take God at His Word, with NO BUTS (JOHN 3: 16-17; HEBREWS 4:16; I PETER 5: 6-7)!

CHAPTER 7

The Number of Completion
GENESIS 2:1-3

The night of my accident, back in 1979, I was with a man I had known and lived with for several years. He was my first true love. Let's call him my special friend. He was the type of man every woman dreams about.

Not only was he tall, brown skinned and handsome, he owned his own business and worked hard in it. He was a team player, affectionate, understanding, and soft spoken, but no punk. He was a giver, protector, a provider and he was a great father figure to my son. He wasn't a Christian, and at that point in my life neither was I.

We also enjoyed the outdoors and each other. This was during the era when everybody owned a van. The vans were painted with murals, like pictures on a wall. We enjoyed music, traveling, and cook-outs with family and friends.

Our love-making was forbidden and truly sin. We would experience ecstasy. The forbidden satisfaction of meeting each other's physical and mental needs bonded us closer. Our fornication was detrimental for me. It led to a strong soul tie which took years of praying to sever.

This man helped me to overcome the low opinion and the low self-esteem I had of myself. He told me I was beautiful, intelligent and he appreciated everything about me.

As a little girl, I was told by my mother I would have big feet and bad skin. Over time, my shoe size did increase. But today, I only wear a size six shoe and the acne on my face has cleared-up. But to my special friend, those things didn't matter.

He loved and wanted me. He even expressed enjoyment in me when he watched me perform my motherly duties such as bathing my son, and especially my conversations with my son while dressing him.

My special friend worked with me to keep our house a home. He would call me at work and tell me he would pick up my son from pre-school and when I got home, my dinner was cooked and on the table. He would mop and wax the floors. He did it all.

In the evening, after my son would go to sleep, we would turn the lights down, turn the music on, smoke a little weed and, based on the song, I would dance for him. He had his own private striper and show girl. Yes! We thought we had everything, but we didn't have Jesus.

It was Flesh vs. Spirit, and at that point in my life, flesh had the upper hand. My heart was hard, I wasn't listening to and didn't want to hear from God. Whenever someone tried to talk to me about Jesus, I would turn off. God's Word fell on stony ground.

As a young child, I had accepted Jesus as my Savior, but I had no teaching. I was not totally committed to God. The Word of God couldn't take root in my heart. But through my upcoming circumstances, God was going to cultivate the soil of my heart and plant His Word in it.

I was young, very selfish and self centered. I was living with the perfect man but inside I was still unhappy. The old saying, you don't miss your water until your well runs dry, is a true statement, and that's where I eventually found myself.

He sincerely loved me and wanted a relationship and a family, but I was too immature and confused to appreciate what I had. The friction and restlessness in me started affecting all parts of our relationship. Our sexual encounters were starting to lack fulfillment.

In order to stimulate our sexual needs, we checked into motels to watch pornography in hopes that the images would stir-up our now dormant passion. It didn't work.

My inner-man, my spirit, needed more and my mortal man, my flesh, wasn't the solution or cure. I started outside relationships with other men under the umbrella of car pooling. To my knowledge, he remained faithful. My sexual appetite for variety was increasing, but I still wanted him.

My special friend had just opened his own upholstery shop and he didn't need my drama or additional stress. We separated but remained distant friends and for a while, each other's booty call.

During our separation he fathered two handsome sons but never married their mother. Our bond was so strong we accepted each others friendship in lieu of physical involvement.

We lived apart for about two and a half years. During the time of our separation, I used men to try to fill the void that actually, only God could fill. I became more promiscuous, a down right "whore!"

Thank God this was before AIDS. I was doing whatever I wanted to do with no strings attached. Don't get it twisted, I only liked men. I was looking for God's love in all the wrong places. In reality, men were not the answer.

One good thing came out of this break up. I made a quality decision to further my education. The decision for me to go back to school was made the morning after a booty-call. My special friend and I were in his bathroom, sitting on the edge of an old fashion bathtub when he asked me, "Olivia, what do you really want to do?" I said, "Dance!" He said, "Then do it!" I cried and he held me in his comforting arms.

In order to dance, I had to sharpen my dance skills and lose some weight. I enrolled in a ballet class and a modern/jazz class. To enter a university for dance, I had to audition. I studied ballet under a master, and that was hard. My height would work against me. I was only five feet two inches tall and this was before the Debbie Allen era.

Even then my special friend was there. One time while I was in class, my car was stolen. I called him and asked if he could pick me up. Of course he said, "Yes." He was my knight in shinning armor.

During the weeks following, I applied to and auditioned for two universities. My first audition was at the California Institute of the Arts otherwise known as Cal Arts. It's one of the finest Universities on the West Coast for the arts.

My cousin wanted to drive me to my audition. When I told my special friend about the audition he offered to drive both of us.

There are no levels for auditions at Cal Arts. Either you have it or you don't. I didn't have it. After my audition, I walked off the dance floor, sat down and started crying. My cousin and special friend came over to console me. I felt a lot better when my cousin told me that I wasn't the first to be removed from the floor. I gathered all of my things together, and we left. On the way home, we stopped to get something to eat. Afterwards he drove us to my cousin's apartment. I thanked him and we said good-bye.

My second audition was successful. I passed the dance audition at California State University Long Beach, but wasn't accepted because in high school, I didn't take the required tests needed for college.

I was disappointed. But by this time, I was attending Monday night Bible Study, so my faith was starting to sprout. I had to get my doctor to put me on disability. I took a medical leave from the County of Los Angeles and later quit. This way I would be eligible to apply for Public Assistance and attend school full time.

I enrolled in Los Angeles Trade Technical Community College with the mind set of completing one semester, then transferring to California State University, Long Beach. In my first semester, I decided to stay at Trade Tech and earn an Associate of Arts Degree. My goal was to teach dance. Trade-Tech offered an Associate Degree in Recreation and I could transfer to a four year university majoring in Physical Education.

After my first semester, the Community College District dropped the Degree in Recreation, so now what do I do? The campus atmosphere was great and the other students and faculty were friendly, so I decided to stay.

I completed all of my general education classes so I could be ready for whatever God had planned for me. During my two years at Trade-Tech, I studied public speaking and competed in various tournaments and earned trophies.

I organized and danced at all the cultural activities and programs on and off campus. I was first runner up in a beauty contest on campus.

The competition was based on departments, not the person. I was the representative for the printing department. But the cosmetology department was larger, so that's why I placed first runner-up. I became very involved with student government, politics and community services.

I had the honor of dancing at the Inaugural Installation of the first African-American President of Los Angeles Trade-Technical College, President Thomas Stevens.

Not only did I graduate with my degree in General Studies, I was nominated and received the Outstanding Young Women of America Award, 1979. I also earned the prestigious, full tuition paid, Norman Topping Student Aid Award Scholarship to the University of Southern California. I decided to major in Psychology.

I was very thankful to God for granting me the scholarship and the opportunity to serve my community. In my final letter as Literary Editor of the Trade-Tech newspaper, *The Trade Winds*, I declared my allegiance to God and my faith in Jesus Christ.

Little did I know I had declared war against Satan and his demons. From that moment on, Satan was out to kill me.

I wasn't going to church regularly, but I faithfully watched Ever Increasing Faith on Sunday mornings. Faith came by hearing and hearing by the Word of God (ROMANS 10:17).

During the summer of my graduation from Trade-Tech, my special friend and I resumed our relationship and were talking about marriage. It started one afternoon when I was visiting him at his apartment.

At this point, our relationship was plutonic. He had his female lovers and I had my male lovers. But the soul tie was still connected, so we became lovers again. The sweet sensation of his body rubbing against mine was breathtaking. But where was my God? Was God with me, in the midst of my sins? God help me!

My first weeks at USC were different. The students were teenagers and most were coming from wealthy and professional homes. Here I was a divorced, single parent on welfare and receiving food stamps. But I was cool. I stayed to myself. That gave me time to read, study and think, not knowing that Satan was actually putting things together for my destruction.

That year, Halloween was a three day weekend. My special friend's van club was invited to a Halloween party. We planned to go and have a good time. The venue had multiple rooms, with a party in each room. The entire location was very festive. I dressed as a woman from outer space.

My hair was styled in the shaped of a helmet and I wore a leotard and tights with high heels. My face was made up with false eye lashes and I made cuffs out of paper for my wrists. As I said, we were planning to have a good time.

I went to the ladies' restroom and while I was fixing my hair, an older lady walked in and she started complementing me on my costume. She asked if I would walk with her so her friends and her husband could see my costume.

I thought that was kind of her, so I agreed. Come to find out, her husband was the deputy who hired me to work for the County of Los Angeles.

I was pleased to give him my testimony. I shared how I was able to take a leave from my job, graduated from Trade-Tech and earned a full tuition scholarship to USC.

He expressed pride in my accomplishments and said he would be proud to assist me in anyway he could in my future endeavors. I thanked him and accepted his card.

Little did I know his wife would later become a good friend, my prayer-partner in Christ and a living example of a godly woman and wife.

After the party, the group decided to go somewhere to eat. We were a large group of approximately sixteen adults. The restaurant we went to was not staffed to accommodate such a large group, so we decided to leave and find another restaurant.

As we were walking out, another man was being escorted out, forcibly. The man was high on a drug called PCP. Earlier, he even tried to sell some of the PCP to one of our friends. They got into an argument and almost fought.

The unruly man walked out first and we slowly strolled out behind him. To get back to where the vans were parked, we had to cross a drive-way which was between the parking lot and the restaurant. The man high on PCP got into his late model car and literally drove into our group. He hit me and another man.

CHAPTER 8

AR-RAHMAN/AR-RAHEEM
My God is Merciful
2 CHRONICLES 30:9

I woke up three days later in the hospital. One of my high school friends heard about the accident and came to see me. She and I had kept in touch over the years. She asked me would it be all right if she invited her cousin to come and see me. I said sure.

She had been trying to get me to meet her cousin for years and when he heard about the accident, he was moved with concern.

He came to see me and we talked for hours. Months later, he told me that he fell in love with me the first time he saw me and that he believed his purpose in my life was to help me get over the death of my father.

Little did I know, not only would he help me through the death of my father, he would become my husband, and his suicide would be the door God would use to manifest His glory in my life.

My high school friend's cousin owned his own car dealership. He and one of his younger brothers would take clients to the car auctions to bid on and purchase cars. His time was somewhat flexible. During my return stay in the hospital, we became good friends.

My special friend, who was now my fiancé, was troubled and with good cause. My fiancé had moved his things in my apartment so he could take care of my son and me.

He would cook breakfast for my son and me and he would serve me before he left for the shop. He would assist my son with getting dressed and take him to school. He would leave his business to pick my son up from school and take him to his shop so I didn't have to worry and I could rest. He did a great job and I was about to thank him with disloyalty and betrayal.

In my heart, I knew my life was changing, I just didn't understand how. I was focused on what I thought was something different and better. I was careless and heartless in how I handled my fiancé's feelings. He didn't deserve to be treated the way I was treating him. All he did was to love me and take care of me.

Later in my life, I was granted the chance to apologize and express my deepest sorrow for what I put him through. I pray that God's plan of salvation be manifested in his life, in Jesus Name. Amen.

Because of my relationship with my high school friend's cousin, my fiancé packed his things and moved out of my apartment. He told me, when he walked out of the door, that he would never take me back. It was over! What about the love? Well, real love never dies.

My new friend was thrilled that my fiancé had moved out. He stepped right in with cooking, cleaning and taking care of my son and me. He asked if he could bring some clothing over and stay the night so it would be easy on him. I said sure. I was getting stronger. My new friend met my family and they liked him. I met his siblings and they liked me, also. One brother openly stated to him, "She's pretty, too," referring to me.

At this point in our relationship, there was no physical touching. I was still under a doctor's care and I was not going to take any risks at all. He went with me and my cousin to the doctor's office for the final visit just to be sure that everything was correct, and everything was.

That night we tried having sex and it worked. The sex was nothing like what I was use to. I didn't know it then, but the soul-tie was still connected and a part of me was being carried in my special friend.

As I got stronger, I could do for myself and walk somewhat on both legs. On one of those good days, I hobbled upstairs into my bedroom. I looked out the window and asked God, "Why didn't You let me die?" God said, "Olivia, you were not ready and I was not finished with you."

I pondered for a moment on what I had just heard, and from that point on, the world looked different and my destiny was set. I purposed in my heart and said with my mouth that I was going to live for God and His glory. I was living in purpose. God's Hand was on me to do good and not evil (II Corinthians 5:17).

I told my new friend that we would have to marry, or he would have to move out. On Saturday, May 24, 1980, we were married.

I wanted to do the right thing and do it the right way. As Christians, we must read and study God's Word to receive understanding of what God's "right thing" and "right way" are for each of our lives. The Word of God is where we all must start (Psalm 111:10; Proverbs 4:10). It's vital for living a successful life. And when we add prayer and intercession to our lives, we are building and fortifying our spirits for obedience and service.

71

My new husband was a good and kind man as well, but I didn't have a clue about his deeply hidden emotional disorders or his drug abuse problem. The question you might ask is, did I seek God on whether I should marry this man or not? The answer to that question is "No!"

Or you may ask if I wanted to be in God's perfect will concerning my recent decisions? That answer is definitely yes.

At this time in my life I did not have a revelation on being unequally yoked (II Corinthians 6:14). But what I finally comprehended was revelation knowledge on FORNICATION AND SEXUAL SIN! No more sex out of marriage for me (I Corinthians 6:18; II Timothy 2:22).

CHAPTER 9

JEHOVAH ROPHE
God is my Healer
EXODUS 15:26

Going back to July 1982, as a result of my husband's suicide, I was forced to think about things and do things I was not accustomed to: food shopping, house cleaning, mopping the floors, taking out trash, even driving. My deceased husband did everything or paid someone to do it for me.

Also, the pain in my left hip was so great that I had to start taking pain pills. Sometimes, the pain was so severe I would go to the bathroom and cry. That was my only release, but the pain grew worse.

My marijuana smoking and taking of pain pills increased, but there was no relief. I knew I couldn't run from my responsibilities.

While watching Christian television, I received the revelation about healing and the manifestation of healing (ISAIAH 53:5).

Faith came, because I embraced the Word in my heart for myself. I thought to myself, "I don't have to live with this pain." God's Word said I was healed. I made up my mind on the upcoming Sunday night, I was going to have my pastor, Pastor Fredrick Price, lay hands on me for prayer of agreement for my healing (PSALMS 6:2; 30:2; 103:1-4).

The first Sunday in August 1982, was Communion Sunday night. All that week, Satan was on his job. The pain was more intense than ever. Every step I took was extremely painful. But, I kept on saying, "Healing belongs to me and I claim it in the Name of Jesus." That Sunday night, I came expecting to receive the full manifestation of healing in my body.

When I arrived at the church, the service had started and people were still standing outdoors waiting to get in somehow. I didn't want to sit in the overflow room. To make sure I was in the atmosphere for healing, I was determined to sit in the main sanctuary. I prayed, "God, please! All I need to do is to get in."

I felt like the woman with the issue of blood, "'If I could only touch the hem of His garment...'"

Miraculously, God answered my prayer. An usher called me specifically and said, "I have a seat for you." Praise God! I was seated in the main sanctuary.

Pastor Price prayed and the congregation took of the bread and the wine. But when I took of the cup and pulled it from my lips, I felt a warm presence, almost like a calming, soothing heat rising up in my body. It started at the top of my head, passed through my shoulders and down through my waist.

I could feel the heat burning through my hip as if the calcium was being dissolved. Praise the Lord. I received my healing. Then I understood what the woman with the issue of blood must have felt, as relief, joy and peace flowed through her. She said, "If I could only. . ." and Jesus said, "Daughter, your faith has made you whole" (MATTHEW 9:27).

Towards the end of the service, Pastor Price called for those who had experienced healing in their bodies to please come forth. So, I did. Praise God, I was healed. I jumped up and down saying, "No more pain." He told us to do something we couldn't do before. Before my healing, I couldn't coordinate a three point turn to the left. Praise God, now I can. I can do all things through Christ Jesus who strengthens me.

This is to the believer, if you are standing for healing, please take your eyes off your need and reach out to help someone else. God's Word, in LUKE 6:38 says, "Give and it shall be given unto you." This scripture is not just for money and finances. In prayer, search your heart and ask God to reveal the sin in your life so that God's Spirit can cleanse you and make you whole.

God wants to develop wholeness in your life. God wants wholeness for you in your spirit, your soul, which is your mind and emotions, and your physical body (PHILIPPIANS 2:12-13; 3:13-14; COLOSSIANS 3:12-16; III JOHN 2).

Praise the Lord! I didn't realize until two weeks later that my left leg had grown out. My son and I were walking and he called to me. "Mommy! Mommy! You're walking too fast. Slow down!"

Glory to God! I was back on top! His mercy endures forever (I CHRONICLES 6:34)! I had everything working on my behalf. Everything was going good. I was going to Bible Study Monday, Tuesday, and Friday nights. My mind was at peace (ISAIAH 26:3). My child care business was prospering and the bills were being paid.

Now, here comes the thief, Satan. What did he want? He wanted what he always wants, our confidence in God's Word. Now remember, if we take our eyes off of God's Word we are setting our selves up for destruction (JOHN 10:10).

Along came distraction and a test in the form of an ex-boy friend who called to express his condolences about my husband's death. He asked if he could come by to see my son and me. He just wanted to see how we were doing. He came over and we talked.

I told him how God was blessing me and how my business was successful and invited him to come go to church with me. He had some off-the-wall reason why he was too busy to visit my church, but that I should visit his church. Eventually, I took him up on his offer just to see where his head was. He was into Science of Mind teaching, which is not the Word of God.

I didn't find out until later he had been my deceased husband's drug dealer; that's how cold blooded he was. His reasoning for selling my deceased husband drugs was he was going to buy it from somebody anyway, so why not him.

Back in the day, he was a high roller, known for his entrepreneurship. He had the best product and was known to hold his own on the street. He was short in height, but not in personality and guts. He introduced me to the Cadillac Seville. He drove the first style in two tones of pink. Whenever I needed his car, it was mine. So when he asked to borrow my Seville, I thought nothing about it. This time, he kept it for days without any word.

One of my neighbors saw my car parked around the corner from my house and called me. I went to see and it was my car. He finally called me and said he knew I would be displeased (ticked-off is more like it) and that's why he parked it there. What I didn't know was that he had started smoking crack.

Crack was the new drug on the streets of Los Angeles at that time, and crack was enslaving everyone who picked it up. He tried to sell crack and smoke it, too. Any street hustler knows you should never consume your own product. He strayed from the rule and started smoking his own merchandise and was battling with addiction.

He took my kindness for weakness and that was the straw that broke this camel's back. So because of his drug involvement and the fact that I couldn't trust him, I backed-off from the relationship.

My advice to everyone is to never take your eyes off of the Lord Jesus Christ and be quick to repent when you stray or disobey. Thank God for His mercy and grace (HEBREWS 4:16).

CHAPTER 10

EL-SHADDAI
God is more than enough
GENESIS 17:1

*B*y now it was about December, 1982. My body was more flexible than even before the accident. I continued to smoke marijuana but believe me, God was dealing with me and that habit. I
was so naïve. I had no solid reason for changing. I would smoke a
joint (marijuana cigarette) and even go to Bible study. Marijuana
was my friend, or was it? Now that I was a member of Crenshaw
Christian Center. I was seriously thinking about becoming a
part of the Helps Ministry (Hebrews 6:10).

One Sunday morning, Pastor Fred Price stepped down from
the pulpit and was walking the floor of the main sanctuary
teaching as he so often would do. This particular Sunday, I was
sitting in the side section of the main sanctuary about three rows
from the aisle. While he was teaching, he walked over and stood
in front of the section where I was sitting. Pastor Price looked
me dead in my eyes and by the Spirit of God said, "If you are
working in the Helps Ministry, you can not smoke marijuana!" I
nodded my head in agreement.

It took me a moment to completely stop smoking. But, when
I made up my mind serving in the church was more important
than getting high, I stopped. Praise God! By the summer of

1983, I had completely given up marijuana and I have had no desire of starting back! Now marijuana has no place in my life. To God be the glory!

In what I describe as my recovery from sin and the deceptions of Satan, I made up my mind nothing or no one was going to stop me from fulfilling the purpose that God had for my life.

My family, at this point, was no real spiritual help to me. They were trying to convince me to give up my home. But I had asked God to allow me to keep my house. I did not want to, and wasn't going to give it up.

Thank God for the Holy Spirit. The Holy Spirit kept me on my course. I knew I couldn't give up because God, through His Son Jesus Christ, had brought me from death to life and I wasn't going to give up anything that God had given me!

What I needed was reinforcement in the area of faith. My family was blind to what I was saying. They really thought I was crazy. My grandmother's beliefs and faith weren't up to the level I needed for my life.

I knew I could receive additional spiritual reinforcement from my church, so I made an appointment with Pastor James Price. At that time, he was one of the assistant pastors at Crenshaw Christian Center. Pastor James Price helped me complete my New Members Class on time. God is so good.

I gave Pastor James a little of my background and stated my reasons for making my appointment. All I needed was someone to stand in agreement with me. That's all I needed. I just needed a prayer partner! I praise God for the Pastoral Staff of Crenshaw Christian Center.

July is a special month for me and my business. Not only because of my Child Care license, but after five years of being exposed to the ministry of Crenshaw Christian Center and Ever

Increasing Faith Television Ministry and following the teaching of the Word of God, July was the month I finally received the Right Hand of Fellowship at Crenshaw Christian Center. All praises to God!

At first, I had to make up my mind what I wanted because a double minded person receives nothing from God (JAMES 1:7-8).

I had to file Chapter 7 bankruptcy to stop the bank from selling my home from under me. After that, a Chapter 13 bankruptcy was filed to set up a payment plan so I could make up the back mortgage payments.

You have to remember, my business is children and the fees from the children was my income, and I needed more income.

I asked Pastor James to stand in agreement with me for financial increase. Increase came and I was able to make my monthly mortgage payments and keep food on the table. To God be the glory!

I had filed a civil law suit following my accident, but nothing came out of it. The entire case was mishandled by my attorney. To make a long story short, I had to file for an appeal as well as filing a Victim of a Violent Crime claim.

I prayed for favor concerning this situation. Even though four and a half years had passed, I was still within the filing deadline for the Victim of a Violent Crime claim. My petition was inspected and granted, praise God, His Word works. The civil case and the appeal were lost. I was denied any compensation from them, but I am totally persuaded I am more than a conqueror. God is a rewarder of them that diligently seek Him (ROMANS 8:37; HEBREWS 11:6).

The fact God gave me my life is my assurance that whatsoever I ask in line with His word, believing in my heart, I shall receive it (MATTHEW 21:21-22).

Two weeks before my bankruptcy court date, Satan, through a so called friend came knocking at my door. DISTRACTION!

He and I had worked together and had not seen each other in years. When we first met, he worked for a law firm and would come to the courthouse where I worked to file papers. We had been lovers and we partied together. When I broke-up with my special friend, he and I hooked up out of pure pleasure.

He was a good sex partner and had a wonderful voice. He sang and played with a band. During the 70s every weekend was a party! After I left the County of Los Angeles and started college, he got married. The one thing I didn't do knowingly was have affairs with married men.

I respected the sanctity of marriage and he wasn't going to lay up in my bed and the bed of his wife, too! So we lost contact with each other. I had to let him know, because he was married, he could not lay up with me anymore. I might be promiscuous, but adultery wasn't going to come back on me. I was no home-wrecker and I knew I would marry again.

Now, four years later, we were re-establishing our friendship but not our sex relationship (ROMANS 1:16-17). He told me he was separated from his wife and he was living with his grand-mother. This might sound funny but I told God if I ever committed fornication, He had permission to take my life, and I meant it from my heart.

We would go to the clubs because he knew I loved to dance. He would stand on the dance floor and watch me dance under the disco lights. I also enjoyed eating Mexican food so he would go shopping and come over to my house and cook for me. We were having a lot of fun. No strings, just friends.

Later in our relationship, he told me he needed to borrow some money to pay his car note. What he withheld from me was his battle with smoking crack. As stated before, crack usage was the start of the fall for the black family. It had a domino effect. Crack took the black woman down to her knees, and you know that takes strength.

I loaned him the money, even though the Holy Spirit warned me not to. Disobedience sucks (I SAMUEL 15:22)! The result of my disobedience was that I lost all but one child from my business. My disobedience had opened the door and let Satan in.

I confessed my sin of disobedience and went to the Word. I just prayed I hadn't blown it completely. The one thing I did learn from this experience was to listen to that still small voice of God's guidance.

I immediately terminated the relationship with him. I prayed, "Lord, please have mercy on me." I JOHN 1:9 says, *If we confess our sins, he is faithful and just to forgive us of our sins, and to cleanse us from all unrighteousness.* PROVERBS 24:16 states *For a righteous man falls seven times and rises again.*

I held on to those Words. I made another appointment with Pastor James Price. I walked into his office, broke down and cried like a baby. He laughed and told me I was just growing. We prayed and agreed for increase. The increase was slow, but increase did come. God is always on time. All I would say was, "Lord, You promised, You promised."

Satan was waging a mental attack on me but I knew what to do. I had to pray in the Holy Spirit. Unless I was having a conversation with the children or another adult, I prayed in the Spirit all the time. God permitted me to flex in my spiritual growth.

What the devil meant for evil, God used it for my good. In the mental attack, I recognized and developed my intercessory skills. As soon as I received the revelation about interceding, the mental attacks stopped (II CORINTHIANS 10: 3-5). In addition to overcoming the mental attacks, I had built up my spirit man (I CORINTHIANS 14: 4). God was growing me up and getting me ready for the next classes, which were men and emotions (JAMES 1:12-14).

God is not the tempter, but like a newborn child, we too, must develop and mature in the things of God!

CHAPTER 11

JEHOVAH ROHI
The Good Shepherd
PSALM 23:1

I started making mortgage payments for July, 1983 which was $740.58 plus back payments to the court trustee of $533.18 each month. This is not including food, phone, water and power, heating, car notes, gas for the car and tithes and offerings.

Praise God! I'm glad God will supply all my need according to His riches and glory through Jesus Christ. All my debt was current. Praise God for the Lord, Jesus Christ and His love.

I look back on it all; my losses, as the result of disobedience, the pain associated with my husband's death, the false accusations, and the emotional trauma caused by making wrong choices.

All I can say is, "At least I didn't have to go to the cross for all mankind." So whatever you are going through, count it all joy (JAMES 1:2-4). Not the experience, but knowing God is with you in the experience, the growth and outcome of the experience!

By this time, my business was going good. My income and giving record was steady. My focus was on God's Word and being obedient to God's Word. I would go out with male, non-Christian friends to concerts and large gatherings but nothing intimate.

Around this time, a lot of the single women at Crenshaw Christian Center were confessing, "I am believing God for my mate". Well, I was not in that crowd. I was content with just God and me.

Little did I know that is where God wants us all to be. God wants us to be totally content and sold out to Him, and I was good with that. I didn't have to worry about anyone's feelings. I didn't have to answer to anyone except God, and I liked it that way. I would take my son and the child care children out on field trips and to the parks and I was having a ball. No worries!

I enjoyed all of the Bible studies at Crenshaw Christian Center, but Monday night Bible Study was my first introduction to the hands-on, prophetic, Word of God, anointed teaching at Crenshaw. This is when Crenshaw Christian Center was actually located on Crenshaw Blvd. and before its move to the Pepperdine University campus.

Monday night Bible study was taught by Beverly "BAM" Crawford. The Bible Study was enjoyable and informative and the prophetic move of the Holy Spirit was always present. For those Monday night Bible Studies, you still had to arrive early if you wanted a good seat. The Bible Study sessions were held in the main sanctuary. This particular Monday night was no different from the rest. I got to church early to get a good seat and have some down-time before the teaching started.

In walked this dark brown complexioned man in his mid thirties, wearing an un-pressed shirt and pants, and needing a hair cut. He asked if he could have a seat. I said sure. So, he sat down. This is just a little side bar. People, we don't know what God has in store for us, so don't be so quick to judge a person by their outward appearance. Another way of saying it is not to judge a book by its cover. That person could easily be a diamond in the raw. And that's what was sitting next to me. A diamond!

A few moments passed and we exchanged names and I gave him a child care flier. He asked if he could call me. I said sure and I said to myself, "No traps for me".

One thing God did drop in my spirit was if I wanted another husband, the man would be older.

Also, I was more attracted to men of dark brown complexion. I told God the only prerequisite I wanted was that my husband would leave me before he would leave God. That week, I didn't hear from the man I met at Bible Study, and that was okay with me.

Monday night Bible Study rolled around and I saw him again. We greeted each other. He told me that he tried to reach me but I had given him the wrong number. I told him to try again.

Finally, that week, we talked. Our conversation was on the Word of God. I wasn't going to miss the mark this time.

When time would permit, I would spend hours studying God's Word and praying. In the afternoon, when the children were taking their naps, I would take the radio out in the back-yard, and turn the music down low to stretch and dance. Every now and then the radio station I listened to, KJLH 102.3 FM, would play a gospel song just for me. That was the icing on the cake.

In my next door neighbor's yard, there was a large avocado tree. In the early mornings, you could hear the birds singing and sometimes in the afternoon they would sing as well. I would pretend I was dancing for the heavenly angels and the children would sit and watch me dance. They really enjoyed my dancing.

I had no understanding about dating and relationships before marriage as a Christian woman, so once again, I went to my church. I called and spoke with the receptionist and asked if she would give me some advice on Christian dating. She agreed. I chose to talk to her because whenever I made my other appointments, she was always helpful and pleasant to talk with.

Her husband, at that time, was an assistant pastor at Crenshaw Christian Center, so we used his office for the session. I told her I knew sex was out, but I wanted to know, "How do Christians date?"

She told me I should only date in a group or go to places where there were other people and I should avoid intimate settings. I asked about clothing.

She said, "Be modest, but not religious." The one thing that I, personally, would add to this is no kissing. Kissing leads to touching and touching can lead to sex and pre-marital sex is sin. I thanked her for her advice and she told me if I had any other questions, to just give her a call.

Weeks passed before my now new friend and I really started talking. One thing was for certain, I was not looking for a husband. I was talking to another brother in Christ at the church and two outside the church, but it wasn't serious talk. My now new friend would call me on the phone and I would be too busy to talk. So he asked if we could meet up at Monday night Bible Study. I said we could.

One afternoon he called me before Bible study and asked if I would go out with him after Bible study and have a cup of coffee and maybe something to eat. I said OK. The conversation and company were delightful. He was quiet but polite. We went to Bob's Big Boy and as time would have it, later in our relationship, that became our after Bible study treat. We would both order a Taco Salad and something to drink.

It might sound simple, but it was proper behavior for Christians. The key here is talking. In our conversations, we established a relationship and exchanged our goals and desires. The friendship stage of any relationship is the foundation for a lasting partnership.

By now it was close to Thanksgiving and my aunt always had a big dinner for the family at her home. I asked my now new friend if he had any plans. He said no. So, I invited him to my aunt's house, and he accepted.

He drove a late model car. We called his car the orange pumpkin. I told him I would rather drive my car. He met me at my house. He wore a nice shirt and tie with a sweater and his hair was freshly cut. Remember, my car is a 1978 powder blue Seville, so he liked that.

Many of my family members were there. As we walked up to my aunt's house, my mother and cousin were standing outside smoking cigarettes. They greeted us and I introduced Charles, which was my now new friend's name, to them and the rest of my family. My aunt was pleased to meet Charles and to see that I was dating.

She was extremely glad that he was a church attending Christian. She said he appeared to be a good man. We had a good time. We took pictures and he really enjoyed my aunt's cooking, especially her homemade, rum, fruitcake.

My aunt owned a one story, side-by-side, duplex on a narrow residential street. It had a front porch that covered the entire front of the house with stairs and a walk-way on both sides. Her front yard was wide, with the biggest bird bath you've ever seen. It was filled with flowers and sat in the middle of the yard. Whenever I would visit her, I was guaranteed to see children playing in the front yards. It was truly a family neighborhood.

In the month of November, Crenshaw Christian Center would have its annual Praise Dinner. This year, I wanted to go and I needed an escort. I asked Charles if he would escort me to the dinner, and of course, he said yes. Although, I had never attended one, I had heard that the Praise Dinners were fabulous.

I didn't want to spend money to buy a new dress so I wore what I had. My attire was black, with a light silver pattern, print, two-piece, top and skirt. I designed the outfit and had it made years BC (before Christ in my life).

The top was appropriate, however the skirt had splits on both sides, and did I mention, it was semi-sheer? In the light, it was see through. When Charles arrived, and took one look at me his face lit up and he had the biggest smile you would ever want to see. He had a beautiful white orchid corsage for me and he placed it on my wrist. I felt like a princess.

Crenshaw Christian Center's music department was ministering at the Praise Dinner and they had reserved tables for the musicians and their guests. Charles, who was a member of the music ministry, and I were running late.

Instead of walking me over to the tables and introducing me to the people there, he pointed me to the tables and went on stage. Well, you know that was no fun for me.

Some would say his behavior was rude and not of a gentleman. I found out, later, that he meant no disrespect. I learned, in time, whenever he's in his element, he's focused and I'm on my own.

The women at the reserved table took one look at me and said this table is reserved for the band. I tried to tell them that I was the date of one of their members, but they didn't care. So I found a table in the back and sat down.

After the music presentation, Charles attempted to join the group at the tables, but where was his date? I watched as he looked around for me. I stood up so he could see me. He walked over, sat down and asked, "Why are you sitting here?"

I told him the ladies at the table said, "No, this table is for the band". We ate dinner, laughed and enjoyed each others company at the back table. I had forgotten how nice it was to go out on a Cinderella date.

Charles was separated from his wife and young daughter. He had filed for divorce but it was not final. Like me, he had been married twice before and he had two older daughters. The oldest was 15 years old, in high school and living with him.

He worked for the U.S. Postal Service as a letter carrier. His work schedule was a rotating off day Monday through Saturday and off on Sundays.

He was 12 years older than I was. He was 5'11" and his skin was chocolate brown and even toned. His arms were strong from carrying the mail bag and he had big muscular legs from all his walking. He almost had a six-pack in his chest. He was thoughtful and on the quite side.

To his advantage, he loved God and God's Word. Sometimes, he would deliver the mail on my block and leave me nice cards or flowers. He was trying hard to get serious, but not me.

Charles' passion was music and his instrument of choice was the tenor saxophone. He was a professional musician. After work on Saturdays, he would join some friends to play his horn. They would rehearse during the year and as a grand finale, the band would sponsor a concert. I was pleased to see him play outside the church. He played in the Crenshaw Christian Center Orchestra and Band. Later he was appointed band director.

I found out he had been in bands, played locally and toured with Ray Charles, Etta James and various Motown artists just to name a few. His past was interesting, but he was more focused on the future, a future with me.

He would say things like, "You're my wife." I would tell him not me. I would say, "I might help you prepare for your wife but I'm not her" (Proverbs 18:22).

He would tell me God told him I was a perfect wife. I would say "Yes, but not yours."

What's not funny is one of my other Christian male friends told me the same thing. He said God told him that I was a perfect wife, but not his, so back off, and he did. Can you see God's Hand moving in my life?

My birthday is Christmas Eve. As Christmas got closer, I didn't have a lot of money, but my son and I always had food to eat. I asked Charles about his plans for Christmas. He told me he hoped to have his younger daughter for the holidays. I suggested, if he would like to, he and his daughters could join my mother, my siblings, my son and me for dinner.

With a big smile on his face he accepted my invitation. About a week before the holiday, he put a check in my mailbox towards the Christmas dinner, which was very considerate of him.

Christmas dinner turned out fantastic. The food was good and everyone ate well. Charles and I were in the kitchen when my mother walked in and asked us the most profound question. She asked us if we were going to get married. And she was stone sober, too.

I looked at her with a blank expression on my face. I couldn't answer yes, and I couldn't say no. Now it was time for me to seek God's Face and ask some questions, because I needed answers.

Charles' daughter and I share December birthdays. I told him how much I enjoyed music by Frankie Beverly and Maze. I also hinted how much I would like to see them in their up coming concert. He smiled and didn't say anything.

One afternoon Charles came over. Nothing was different about his stopping by with a surprise. We were sitting and talking when he gave me a card. I opened the envelope, pulled out the card and in it were three tickets for Frankie Beverly and Maze. I screamed and thanked him for my gift. This surprise from Charles was just the beginning of his many more surprises and gifts to come.

He took his oldest daughter and me out for dinner and then to the concert. This was my first time seeing Frankie Beverly and Maze in concert. The music was so good! When they started singing "Joy and Pain," I couldn't stay in my seat. I jumped up and started dancing in the aisle.

I was not concerned with who was watching, the music touched my soul. At the end of the song the people applauded my dancing.

Pause!

It was a weekend afternoon and no one was home; no child care children and my son was visiting relatives. I was sitting in my bedroom praying. My praise was high and I could sense God's presence in the room. God told me, "Look at Charles. Look at him. See what I see."

No one was in the room, so I closed my eyes and I saw in the spirit. I saw the future. I saw Charles standing tall in a well tailored suit in front of a large group of people. My interpretation of the vision was longevity, prosperity, wholeness and success. God said, "By faith, you will get there; trust Me".

I agreed to accept Charles as my husband. I said nothing to him because the Word of God says, "He who finds a wife finds a good thing" (PROVERB 18:22). From this point on, I started looking at Charles differently.

God knew, deep in my heart, I desired a husband, but a husband was not my motivation. Serving God was. I had the revelation of, "Seek ye first the kingdom of God and God's righteousness" (MATTHEW 6:33). I had the revelation of, "No good thing will God withhold from those that walk upright before Him" (PSALMS 84:11).

Being in God's perfect will was most important to me. When it came to men, I had made enough mistakes in my life for two women and I wasn't going down that road anymore.

While the Spirit of God was working with me, the Spirit of God was working with Charles as well. Now, I could sense a softness and compassion in me bonding us together. We purposed in our hearts to follow the leading of the Holy Spirit.

Charles would come by everyday after work and I would have dinner prepared. He would eat at my house or he would call me ahead of time and ask if I wanted something special to eat. We would study the Word of God together, watch television and listen to music.

We started doing things together as a family as well; such things as going to Sunday services, going to the park, and attending movies. We wanted our children to become friends at their own pace.

The youngest was quite and shy but his oldest and my son clicked. They had a lot in common including music and movies. This is an important part of transitioning and bringing a blended family together. The children must buy into the vision and direction that God has for the family. Without this blending of the family, the children will become a crack for Satan to enter in and cause havoc in the marriage.

One evening, we were in my living room standing in front of the fireplace. Charles got down on one knee and proposed. It wasn't a surprise. We both knew God had granted us to marry, so it was just a matter of time. Charles gave me a promise ring.

His birthstone is pearl so that was the stone in the ring. Two months later, he gave me a beautiful, diamond engagement ring. In the spirit, we knew God had joined us together. We also knew things MUST be done decently and in order. We knew not to jump the gun as far as sex was concerned.

Even if you both know God has granted you to marry, don't step into sexual sin, because the sin could open the door for death and destruction of the marriage.

It was only after Charles and I knew we were to marry, that we embraced and kissed as a man and woman. We purposed in our hearts to do this God's way, which meant, no premarital sex. And, believe it or not, Praise God, we did it God's way (I CORINTHIANS 14:40).

We consummated our marriage on our wedding night. This was the ultimate level of trusting God. For those who say it can not be done, you are a chicken! God will always give you what you need, not necessarily what you think you want. Remember, wants are always subject to change just like fashions!

As we seek God through Jesus Christ, God will then give you the desires of your heart. And baby, you better believe that God made sure that Charles knew all the right buttons to push and pop! Our love making was GOOD!

Pause!

Now that we were engaged to be married, we needed a house. Charles offered to help me get caught up on my delinquent house note and we could live there. I told him no. I wanted a new house to go with my new husband. The Word says not to put new wine into old skins (MATTHEW 9:17). I wanted a totally new beginning. So the hunt was on for the new house.

What I'm about to say, some would disagree with, but God was leading our lives. Do not get it twisted! These were our personal instructions from God and they are not an example for others to follow except for the fact of listening to God.

Remember, I had to file bankruptcy so my credit was no good. We had to purchase a house in Charles' name only. My sister told us about a program that was affordable and that would build you a brand new house. We looked into the possibilities. It was perfect for us. The program worked like this:

It was governed by a non-profit organization. This organization acquired vacant lots all over the city of Los Angeles, and would build three bedroom, one and a half bath, two car attached garage family homes on these lots.

There were four different styles to choose from. Buyers were able to select the color of the rugs and the color of the floor tile. The house came with a built-in range and dishwasher. The program landscaped the front yard and fenced in the back.

By putting our monies together, God made it possible for Charles and me to save up $10,000.00 in three months time. Don't forget, we were still tithing and giving.

We looked at lots and neighborhoods all over southeast Los Angeles. We wanted a large lot so we chose one. We really didn't like the area, but time was running out.

We inquired about delinquent properties people had started to build and backed-out, and as God would have it, there were two houses available. We made an appointment to view them.

The houses were around the corner from each other. One was in the middle of the block and the other was a corner house across the street from the freeway. I told Charles, "Oh no, not the freeway again." He agreed, so we chose the property in the middle of the block.

We prayed about the house and as we were driving away from the house, I got a check in my spirit. I told Charles that was not our house, but the house on the corner, by the freeway, was the one. As we drove around the corner to the other house, a peace rose up in me. Being next to the freeway again wasn't important to me, our being in God's perfect will for our lives was. So the house next to the freeway was it!

We were unable to see, at this point, God's purpose for giving us this house, but we found out later, this house would put us in position to be relocated into a bigger house in a better neighborhood. So it is most important, with no questions asked, you hear the voice of God and follow God's leading (JOHN 10:4-5)!

When the house was finished and ready for us to move in, Charles and I were not married. On the fifth of June, my son, my soon to be daughter and I moved into the house. Charles didn't move in until after we were married.

We wanted to avoid the appearance of sin and not to give any place to the devil (I THESSALONIANS 5:22). We were doing it completely God's way! All the way!

When I told my father's other sister, a so called born again, spirited filled Christian, that I was going to get married and we had not had sex, she asked me how I was going buy a pair of shoes without first trying them on. I told her I walk by faith and not by sight. I was trusting God.

Remember, I was the "catalog queen." I had no fear about buying things "sight unseen." What I feared most, was the possibility of not paying attention when God was trying to lead.

Before moving into my new home, I told the bankruptcy court I was going to move. So the bankruptcy payments I was supposed to make went towards the purchase of our new home as well.

Two days before my moving date, an agent from the bank came to my door. I could see the apprehension in the man's face. He didn't know what to expect. Standing at my door, was a little white man in an all black neighborhood. Much to his surprise, I met him with a smile. He introduced himself and stated his purpose. Before he could put the eviction papers in my hand, I told him I was moving in two days into my new home with my new husband. His face turned red. He broke out in a big smile and wished me much success in my new life. I thanked him, closed the door and gave God praise.

As I looked at those eviction papers he placed in my hand I said out loud, "Not for the King's daughter! I will be walking away with my head held high. To God be the glory! I will tell everyone, 'Trust God' (ROMANS 8:1)!"

Charles and I spent our combined money on the purchase of our new house, so we didn't plan for a traditional wedding. I wanted Pastor James Price to perform the ceremony and Charles agreed. We planned to have an office wedding and decided on Friday, June 22, 1984. Our children were too young to stand in as witnesses, so we asked two of Charles' friends from church to stand in.

The night before the wedding, one of my younger cousins came by and brought me a beautiful beige slip and camisole set as a gift. We talked briefly about my excitement and my new life. I thanked her and told her her gift would be my something new. My something borrowed was my sister's dress. After she left, I gave myself a manicure, a pedicure and pressed, styled and rolled my hair. I got into my bed knowing this would be my last night sleeping alone. I was entering into a new covenant with God and Charles.

Charles gave me his mother's wedding rings as a wedding gift, so I wore the rings for my something old and my something blue were the flowers in my bouquet.

I prayed and thanked God for the privilege and honor of being His daughter and a co-laborer with Jesus Christ. I promised God I would give my all to this marriage and I would totally yield myself to serve and fulfill the call God had on my life.

Our wedding appointment was 10:00 a.m. I had my son and Charles' daughter with me. Both children were dressed in their best. Our colors were beige and blue. Charles met us at the church with his two friends. Charles was very handsome and radiant. He wore a powder blue shirt, and dark blue slacks, navy blue shoes, a tie with matching handkerchief and a beige sports jacket. As I sat in the reception area, waiting for the moment, our First Lady, Dr. Betty Price passed through and gave me words of encouragement as a mother would do. My wedding day was perfect.

After the ceremony, our witnesses dropped the oldest daughter off at her mother's for the weekend and my son went to his great aunt's house. We had the whole house to ourselves and we made good use of it. Praise God everything fit and worked.

It was fantastic. Now I was making love. We were in God's perfect will for our lives with a prosperous future in store. I went from husband to husband with no sin in between. Two and a half years and NO FORNICATION! My God is a keeping God!

Also, after the ceremony, we went outdoors into the garden area and took pictures. It was a beautiful day. The sky was clear and God's glory was shinning on us as well as in us. My husband Charles and I were and are to this day, truly a love story.

The Beginning

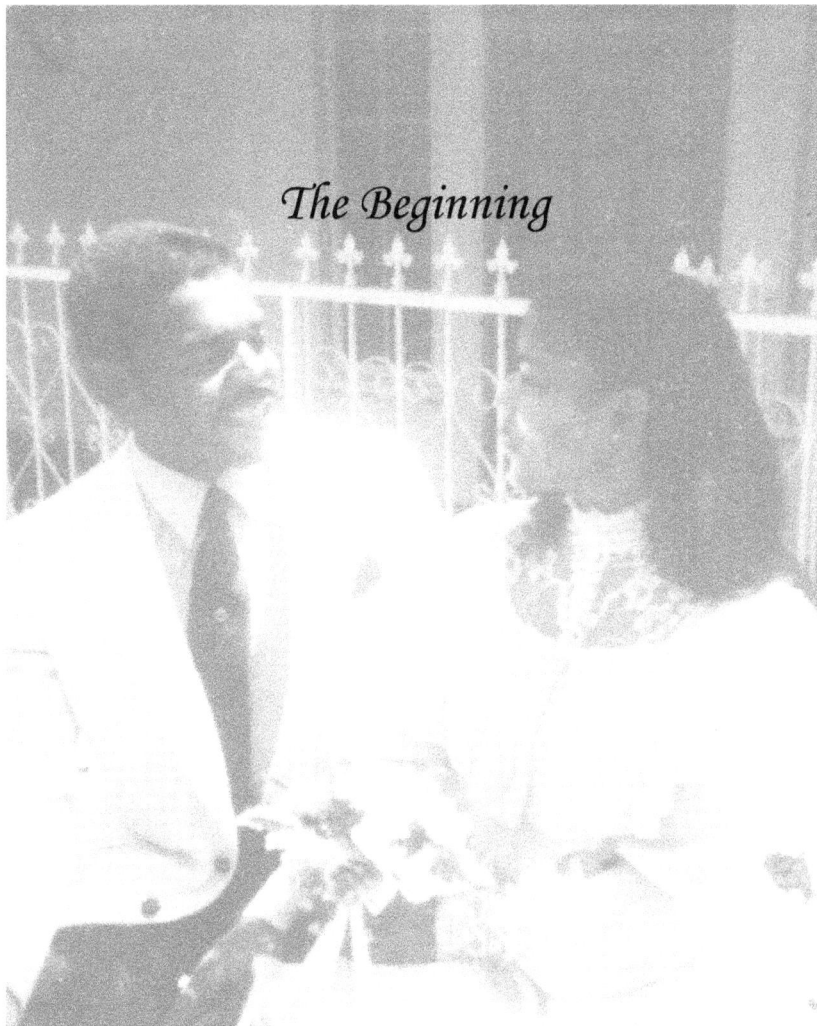

Epilog

This part of my journey of faith has been bittersweet. My understanding of the principals of faith and the process of growth in the Word of God have enabled me to maintain my sanity and touch the lives of thousands.

For me, God's Word, together with loving and serving humanity, is real and everything else is unimportant.

People travel and search the world in order to find themselves. I thank my Heavenly Father through Jesus Christ that I didn't have to make that trip.

God's Word and plan of salvation have made available and granted me to live in happiness, joy and peace along with eternal life.

Riches and total prosperity are in my life because of God's Word and my obedience to that Word.

Thank you Dr. Price.

Scripture References

All scripture references are taken from the King James Version of the Bible unless otherwise stated.

INTRODUCTION
Page xii

> PSALMS 34:8 *O taste and see that the Lord is good: blessed is the man that trusteth in him.*

CHAPTER 1
Page 1

> JUDGES 6:24 *Then Gideon built an altar there unto the Lord, and called it Jehovah-shalom: unto this day it is yet in Ophrah of the Abi-ezrites.*

Page 12

> 2 COR 5:8 *We are confident, I say, and willing rather to be absent from the body, and to be present with the Lord.*

Page 13

> HEB 13:5 *Let your conversation be without covetousness; and be content with such things as ye have: for he hath said, I will never leave thee, nor forsake thee.*

Page 14

> 2 SAM 22:2 *And he said, The Lord is my rock, and my fortress, and my deliverer;*

> MATT 12:34 *O generation of vipers, how can ye, being evil, speak good things? for out of the abundance of the heart the mouth speaketh.*

Page 17

    Psalm 37:23, 24 *²³The steps of a good man are ordered by the Lord: and he delighteth in his way. ²⁴Though he fall, he shall not be utterly cast down: for the Lord upholdeth him with his hand.*

CHAPTER 2
Page 19

    Jeremiah 23:6 *In his days Judah shall be saved, and Israel shall dwell safely: and this is his name whereby he shall be called, THE LORD OUR RIGHTEOUSNESS.*

Page 20

    Phil 4:19 *But my God shall supply all your need according to his riches in glory by Christ Jesus.*

Page 26

    Eph 6:11 *Put on the whole armour of God, that ye may be able to stand against the wiles of the devil.*

CHAPTER 3
Page 29

    Genesis 22:14 *And Abraham called the name of that place Jehovah-jireh: as it is said to this day, In the mount of the Lord it shall be seen.*

    Luke 11:9 *And I say unto you, Ask, and it shall be given you; seek, and ye shall find; knock, and it shall be opened unto you.*

Page 31

    2 Cor 12:9-10 *⁹And he said unto me, My grace is sufficient for thee: for my strength is made perfect in weakness. Most gladly therefore will I rather glory in my infirmities, that the power of Christ may rest upon me. ¹⁰Therefore I take pleasure in infirmities, in reproaches, in necessities, in persecutions, in distresses for Christ's sake: for when I am weak, then am I strong.*

Page 33

1 JOHN 4:4 *Ye are of God, little children, and have overcome them: because greater is he that is in you, than he that is in the world.*

EPH 6:13-14 *13 Wherefore take unto you the whole armour of God, that ye may be able to withstand in the evil day, and having done all, to stand. 14 Stand therefore, having your loins girt about with truth, and having on the breastplate of righteousness;*

CHAPTER 4

Page 35

LEVITICUS 20:7-8 *7 Sanctify yourselves therefore, and be ye holy: for I am the Lord your God. 8 And ye shall keep my statutes, and do them: I am the Lord which sanctify you.*

Page 38

2 COR 9:6 *But this I say, He which soweth sparingly shall reap also sparingly; and he which soweth bountifully shall reap also bountifully.*

GAL 6:7 *Be not deceived; God is not mocked: for whatsoever a man soweth, that shall he also reap.*

MAL 3:10-11 *10 Bring ye all the tithes into the storehouse, that there may be meat in mine house, and prove me now herewith, saith the Lord of hosts, if I will not open you the windows of heaven, and pour you out a blessing, that there shall not be room enough to receive it. 11 And I will rebuke the devourer for your sakes, and he shall not destroy the fruits of your ground; neither shall your vine cast her fruit before the time in the field, saith the Lord of hosts.*

Page 40

1 COR 2:9 *But as it is written, Eye hath not seen, nor ear heard, neither have entered into the heart of man, the things which God hath prepared for them that love him.*

EPH 3:20 *Now unto him that is able to do exceeding abundantly above all that we ask or think, according to the power that worketh in us,*

Page 41

> PROV 3:5-6 *⁵Trust in the Lord with all thine heart; and lean not unto thine own understanding. ⁶In all thy ways acknowledge him, and he shall direct thy paths.*

> HEB 11:6 *But without faith it is impossible to please him: for he that cometh to God must believe that he is, and that he is a rewarder of them that diligently seek him.*

> 2 TIM 1:7 *For God hath not given us the spirit of fear; but of power, and of love, and of a sound mind.*

> 2 CORINTHIANS 5:8 *We are confident, I say, and willing rather to be absent from the body, and to be present with the Lord.*

Page 42

> PROV 3:24 *When thou liest down, thou shalt not be afraid: yea, thou shalt lie down, and thy sleep shall be sweet.*

CHAPTER 5

Page 43

> EZEKIEL 48:35 *It was round about eighteen thousand measures: and the name of the city from that day shall be, The Lord is there.*

Page 44

> JOHN 12:32 *And I, if I be lifted up from the earth, will draw all men unto me.*

Page 45

> PROV 3:25-26 *²⁵Be not afraid of sudden fear, neither of the desolation of the wicked, when it cometh. ²⁶For the Lord shall be thy confidence, and shall keep thy foot from being taken.*

Page 47

> PS 30:10-12 *¹⁰Hear, O Lord, and have mercy upon me: Lord, be thou my helper. ¹¹Thou hast turned for me my mourning into dancing: thou hast put off my sackcloth, and girded me with gladness; ¹²To the end that my*

glory may sing praise to thee, and not be silent. O Lord my God, I will give thanks unto thee for ever.

Page 48

Rom 6:23 *For the wages of sin is death; but the gift of God is eternal life through Jesus Christ our Lord.*

Page 51

Heb 12:1 *Wherefore seeing we also are compassed about with so great a cloud of witnesses, let us lay aside every weight, and the sin which doth so easily beset us, and let us run with patience the race that is set before us,*

Chapter 6

Page 53

Exodus 17:15 *And Moses built an altar, and called the name of it Jehovah-nissi:*

Page 56

1 Cor 3:16 *Know ye not that ye are the temple of God, and that the Spirit of God dwelleth in you?*

1 Cor 6:13 *Meats for the belly, and the belly for meats: but God shall destroy both it and them. Now the body is not for fornication, but for the Lord; and the Lord for the body.*

1 Cor 6:15-20 *[15]Know ye not that your bodies are the members of Christ? shall I then take the members of Christ, and make them the members of an harlot? God forbid. [16]What? know ye not that he which is joined to an harlot is one body? for two, saith he, shall be one flesh. [17]But he that is joined unto the Lord is one spirit. [18]Flee fornication. Every sin that a man doeth is without the body; but he that committeth fornication sinneth against his own body. [19]What? know ye not that your body is the temple of the Holy Ghost which is in you, which ye have of God, and ye are not your own? [20]For ye are bought with a price: therefore glorify God in your body, and in your spirit, which are God's.*

ROMANS 10:9-10 *⁹That if thou shalt confess with thy mouth the Lord Jesus, and shalt believe in thine heart that God hath raised him from the dead, thou shalt be saved. ¹⁰For with the heart man believeth unto righteousness; and with themouth confession is made untosalvation.*

Page 58

JOHN 3:16-17 *¹⁶For God so loved the world, that he gave his only begotten Son, that whosoever believeth in him should not perish, but have everlasting life. ¹⁷For God sent not his Son into the world to condemn the world; but that the world through him might be saved.*

1 PETER 2:9 *But ye are a chosen generation, a royal priesthood, an holy nation, a peculiar people; that ye should shew forth the praises of him who hath called you out of darkness into his marvellous light:*

Ps 37:18-19 *¹⁸The Lord knoweth the days of the upright: and their inheritance shall be for ever. ¹⁹They shall not be ashamed in the evil time: and in the days of famine they shall be satisfied.*

Page 60

JOHN 3:16-17 *¹⁶For God so loved the world, that he gave his only begotten Son, that whosoever believeth in him should not perish, but have everlasting life. ¹⁷For God sent not his Son into the world to condemn the world; but that the world through him might be saved.*

HEB 4:16 *Let us therefore come boldly unto the throne of grace, that we may obtain mercy, and find grace to help in time of need.*

1 PETER 5:6-7 *⁶Humble yourselves therefore under the mighty hand of God, that he may exalt you in due time: ⁷Casting all your care upon him; for he careth for you.*

CHAPTER 7

Page 61

GENESIS 2:1-3 *¹Thus the heavens and the earth were finished, and all the host of them. ²And on the seventh day God ended his work which he had made; and he rested on the seventh day from all his work which he had made. ³And God blessed the seventh day, and sanctified it:*

because that in it he had rested from all his work which God created and made.

Page 66

ROM 10:17 *So then faith cometh by hearing, and hearing by the word of God.*

CHAPTER 8

Page 69

2 CHRONICLES 30:9 *For if ye turn again unto the Lord, your brethren and your children shall find compassion before them that lead them captive, so that they shall come again into this land: for the Lord your God is gracious and merciful, and will not turn away his face from you, if ye return unto him.*

Page 71

2 COR 5:17 *Therefore if any man be in Christ, he is a new creature: old things are passed away; behold, all things are become new.*

PS 111:10 *The fear of the Lord is the beginning of wisdom: a good understanding have all they that do his commandments: his praise endureth for ever.*

PROV 4:10 *Hear, O my son, and receive my sayings; and the years of thy life shall be many.*

Page 72

2 COR 6:14 *Be ye not unequally yoked together with unbelievers: for what fellowship hath righteousness with unrighteousness? and what communion hath light with darkness?*

1 COR 6:18 *Flee fornication. Every sin that a man doeth is without the body; but he that committeth fornication sinneth against his own body.*

2 TIM 2:22 *Flee also youthful lusts: but follow righteousness, faith, charity, peace, with them that call on the Lord out of a pure heart.*

CHAPTER 9
Page 73

EXODUS 15:26 *And said, If thou wilt diligently hearken to the voice of the Lord thy God, and wilt do that which is right in his sight, and wilt give ear to his commandments, and keep all his statutes, I will put none of these diseases upon thee, which I have brought upon the Egyptians: for I am the Lord that healeth thee.*

ISA 53:5 *But he was wounded for our transgressions, he was bruised for our iniquities: the chastisement of our peace was upon him; and with his stripes we are healed.*

PS 6:2 *Have mercy upon me, O Lord; for I am weak: O Lord, heal me; for my bones are vexed.*

PS 30:2 *O Lord my God, I cried unto thee, and thou hast healed me.*

PS 103:1-4 *¹Bless the Lord, O my soul: and all that is within me, bless his holy name. ²Bless the Lord, O my soul, and forget not all his benefits: ³Who forgiveth all thine iniquities; who healeth all thy diseases; ⁴Who redeemeth thy life from destruction; who crowneth thee with loving-kindness and tender mercies;*

Page 74

MATT 9:21 *For she said within herself, if I may but touch his garment, I shall be whole.*

Page 75

LUKE 6:38 *Give, and it shall be given unto you; good measure, pressed down, and shaken together, and running over, shall men give into your bosom. For with the same measure that ye mete withal it shall be measured to you again.*

PHIL 2:12-13 *¹² Wherefore, my beloved, as ye have always obeyed, not as in my presence only, but now much more in my absence, work out your own salvation with fear and trembling. ¹³ For it is God which worketh in you both to will and to do of his good pleasure.*

PHIL 3:13-14 *¹³Brethren, I count not myself to have apprehended: but this one thing I do, forgetting those things which are behind, and reaching forth unto those things which are before, ¹⁴I press toward the mark for the prize of the high calling of God in Christ Jesus.*

COL 3:12-16 *¹²Put on therefore, as the elect of God, holy and beloved, bowels of mercies, kindness, humbleness of mind, meekness, longsuffering; ¹³Forbearing one another, and forgiving one another, if any man have a quarrel against any: even as Christ forgave you, so also do ye. ¹⁴And above all these things put on charity, which is the bond of perfectness. ¹⁵And let the peace of God rule in your hearts, to the which also ye are called in one body; and be ye thankful. ¹⁶Let the word of Christ dwell in you richly in all wisdom; teaching and admonishing one another in psalms and hymns and spiritual songs, singing with grace in your hearts to the Lord.*

3 JOHN 2 *Beloved, I wish above all things that thou mayest prosper and be in health, even as thy soul prospereth.*

1 CHRON 16:34 *O give thanks unto the Lord; for he is good; for his mercy endureth for ever.*

ISA 26:3 *Thou wilt keep him in perfect peace, whose mind is stayed on thee: because he trusteth in thee.*

JOHN 10:10 *The thief cometh not, but for to steal, and to kill, and to destroy: I am come that they might have life, and that they might have it more abundantly.*

Page 77

HEBREWS 4:16 *Let us therefore come boldly unto the throne of grace, that we may obtain mercy, and find grace to help in time of need.*

CHAPTER 10
Page 79

GENESIS 17:1 *And when Abram was ninety years old and nine, the Lord appeared to Abram, and said unto him, I am the Almighty God; walk before me, and be thou perfect.*

115

HEB 6:10 *For God is not unrighteous to forget your work and labour of love, which ye have shewed toward his name, in that ye have ministered to the saints, and do minister.*

Page 81

JAMES 1:7-8 *⁷For let not that man think that he shall receive any thing of the Lord ⁸A double minded man is unstable in all his ways.*

ROM 8:37 *Nay, in all these things we are more than conquerors through him that loved us.*

Hebrews 11:6 *But without faith it is impossible to please him: for he that cometh to God must believe that he is, and that he is a rewarder of them that diligently seek him.*

MATT 21:21-22 *²¹Jesus answered and said unto them, Verily I say unto you, If ye have faith, and doubt not, ye shall not only do this which is done to the fig tree, but also if ye shall say unto this mountain, Be thou removed, and be thou cast into the sea; it shall be done. ²²And all things, whatsoever ye shall ask in prayer, believing, ye shall receive.*

Page 82

ROM 1:16-17 *¹⁶For I am not ashamed of the gospel of Christ: for it is the power of God unto salvation to every one that believeth; to the Jew first, and also to the Greek. ¹⁷For therein is the righteousness of God revealed from faith to faith: as it is written, The just shall live by faith.*

Page 83

1SAM 15:22 *And Samuel said, Hath the Lord as great delight in burnt offerings and sacrifices, as in obeying the voice of the Lord? Behold, to obey is better than sacrifice, and to hearken than the fat of rams*

1JOHN 1:9 *If we confess our sins, he is faithful and just to forgive us our sins, and to cleanse us from all unrighteousness.*

PROV 24:16 *For a just man falleth seven times, and riseth up again: but the wicked shall fall into mischief.*

Page 84

2COR 10:3-5 *³For though we walk in the flesh, we do not war after the flesh: ⁴(For the weapons of our warfare are not carnal, but mighty through God to the pulling down of strong holds;) ⁵Casting down imaginations, and every high thing that exalteth itself against the knowledge of God, and bringing into captivity every thought to the obedience of Christ;*

2COR 14:4 *He that speaketh in an unknown tongue edifieth himself; but he that prophesieth edifieth the church.*

JAMES 1:12-14 *¹²Blessed is the man that endureth temptation: for when he is tried, he shall receive the crown of life, which the Lord hath promised to them that love him. ¹³Let no man say when he is tempted, I am tempted of God: for God cannot be tempted with evil, neither tempteth he any man: ¹⁴But every man is tempted, when he is drawn away of his own lust, and enticed.*

CHAPTER 11

Page 85

PSALM 23:1 *The Lord is my shepherd; I shall not want.*

JAMES 1:2-4 *²My brethren, count it all joy when ye fall into divers temptations; ³Knowing this, that the trying of your faith worketh patience. ⁴But let patience have her perfect work, that ye may be perfect and entire, wanting nothing.*

Page 92

PROV 18:22 *Whoso findeth a wife findeth a good thing, and obtaineth favour of the Lord.*

Page 94

PROV 18:22 *Whoso findeth a wife findeth a good thing, and obtaineth favour of the Lord.*

MATT 6:33 *But seek ye first the kingdom of God, and his righteousness; and all these things shall be added unto you.*

Ps 84:11   *For the Lord God is a sun and shield: the Lord will give grace and glory: no good thing will he withhold from them that walk uprightly.*

Page 95

1 Cor 14:40   *Let all things be done decently and in order.*

Page 97

Matt 9:17   *Neither do men put new wine into old bottles: else the bottles break, and the wine runneth out, and the bottles perish: but they put new wine into new bottles, and both are preserved.*

Page 98

John 10:4-5   *⁴And when he putteth forth his own sheep, he goeth before them, and the sheep follow him: for they know his voice. ⁵And a stranger will they not follow, but will flee from him: for they know not the voice of strangers.*

1 Thess 5:22   *Abstain from all appearance of evil.*

Page 99

Rom 8:1   *There is therefore now no condemnation to them which are in Christ Jesus, who walk not after the flesh, but after the Spirit.*

About the Author

OLIVIA THOMPSON GREEN was born in Chicago, Illinois. Her family moved to Los Angeles, California when she was six years old. She graduated from Los Angeles High School, Los Angeles Trade-Technical College and earned a full-tuition scholarship to the University of Southern California, majoring in Psychology. She received an Honorary Doctorate Degree in Religious Humanities from St. Stevens Bible College.

Dr. Green is the founder and CEO of Families Working Together Child Care Center & Family Support Services, Inc. (FWT) A 501(c)(3) non-profit community-based organization that provides leadership, entrepreneurial and other educational programs for children 5 to 17 years of age. Other FWT programs include Always Abounding Emergency Family Shelter for women and their children and Rebuilding Lives Community Living and Mentoring Program for men. Both programs provide housing, case management, counseling and permanent housing referrals.

With over thirty years of experience as a successful entrepreneur, educator and community advocate for families, today, Dr. Green serves as a member of the Board of Directors for Community Childcare Collaborative, Inc. and Kingdom Builders. Dr. Green continues to manage and direct, with excellence, Green's 24hr Family Child Care, Inc. She and her husband Charles are members of Crenshaw Christian Center in Los Angeles California.

Dr. Green enjoys Word-filled music, ministering in dance, writing, studying the Word of God and is a committed intercessor. She looks forward to attending the annual conference of the Congressional Black Caucus in Washington, D.C., spending time with family members and going on cruises with her husband. Dr. Green is sold out to fulfilling the purpose that God has for her life.

For additional information on up coming books and booking speaking engagements, please contact us at (323) 293-1991 or www.otgreen.net